C. W. Brister, PhD

MW00466877

Spiritual Wisdom
for Successful Retirement
Living Forward

Pre-publication
REVIEWS,
COMMENTARIES,
EVALUATIONS . . .

"This book is a wholesome package of how-to and inspiration, realism and hope, and timely insight that offers a must-read resource for life in retirement. *Spiritual Wisdom for Successful Retirement* invites retirees, those about to retire, and caregivers to explore what it takes to retire with a measure of success. At the heart of the book is a strong desire: that the reader will be able to live with vitality, usefulness, and hopefulness to a ripe old age.

The reader will meet people who are up to their elbows in life. From the natural order and from human experience, Brister harvests images and insights that offer wisdom for living forward in retirement. He brings a lifetime of work in the field of pastoral care to the challenges of retirement and invites his readers to mine those resources. Retir-

ees and caregivers will find each chapter laden with insight and practical help and wrapped up with a summary of key points.

Hope permeates the pages of *Spiritual Wisdom for Successful Retirement* and leads the reader into a hope-full journey with the gifts and crises, hopes and fears, and limitations and possibilities that accompany retirement. This book is an invaluable tool for ministers who serve among retirees and parishioners who want to make the most of life after career. Those who want to examine issues related to retirees and retirement will find a reservoir that yields fresh help with each reading."

N. Larry Baker, ThD
Senior Minister, First Baptist Church
Sun City West, Arizona

"**A**s a pre-retiree and a clinical gerontologist I deeply appreciate Dr. Brister's latest contribution from both a personal and professional perspective. *Spiritual Wisdom for Successful Retirement* is a well-balanced biopsychosocial-spiritual approach to preparing for generous and optimistic living in all the events of later life, whether one is active or frail.

Each chapter is chock-full of practical information and inspiring reflection. A major strength is the variety of case reports—narratives—that provide the reader with clear examples of the author's teaching points. Of particular help is Dr. Brister's discussion of the challenges of managing time and commitments after retirement so that one does not waste valuable life on inconsequential matters and can remain free to contribute in one's most unique way.

This book can be equally well used by individuals on the verge of retirement, those already experiencing retirement, and counselors, spiritual directors, and pastoral care providers who are helping elders to move forward into new adventures."

Jane M. Thibault, MSSW, PhD
*Associate Clinical Professor
and Clinical Gerontologist
Department of Family
and Geriatric Medicine,
School of Medicine,
University of Louisville,
Louisville, Kentucky*

"**T**his book accomplishes a rare feat. Dr. Brister combines the practical issues of retirement with the spiritual wisdom he garnered through a lifetime of service to others as an academic in ministry. He reminds us that we do not simply retire from a job or a career, we retire *to* . . . something, and it is this 'something' for which we have to plan.

Although current theories of aging discuss positive aspects of aging, the subject of much gerontological literature concerns managing the decline of old age. *Spiritual Wisdom for Successful Retirement* reminds readers that the boundary of a life is not in a body and its physical end, but is that which places limits on our goals in life and hides a view of our final destination."

Helen K. Black, PhD
*Center for Applied Research
on Aging and Health,
Thomas Jefferson University
Philadelphia, Pennsylvania*

The Haworth Pastoral Press®
An Imprint of The Haworth Press
New York • London • Oxford

Spiritual Wisdom
for Successful Retirement
Living Forward

THE HAWORTH PASTORAL PRESS®
Rev. James W. Ellor, DMin, DCSW, CGP
Melvin A. Kimble, PhD
Co-Editors in Chief

Aging and Spirituality: Spiritual Dimensions of Aging Theory, Research, Practice, and Policy edited by David O. Moberg

Wu Wei, Negativity, and Depression: The Principle of Non-Trying in the Practice of Pastoral Care by Siroj Sorajjakool

Pastoral Care to Muslims: Building Bridges by Neville A. Kirkwood

Health Through Faith and Community: A Study Resource for Christian Communities to Promote Personal and Social Well-Being by Edward R. Canda, Aaron Ketchell, Phillip Dybicz, Loretta Pyles, and Holly Nelson-Becker

Spiritual Wisdom for Successful Retirement: Living Forward by C. W. Brister

Spiritual Wisdom
for Successful Retirement
Living Forward

C. W. Brister, PhD

The Haworth Pastoral Press®
An Imprint of The Haworth Press
New York • London • Oxford

For more information on this book or to order, visit
http://www.haworthpress.com/store/product.asp?sku=5537

or call 1-800-HAWORTH (800-429-6784) in the United States and Canada
or (607) 722-5857 outside the United States and Canada

or contact orders@HaworthPress.com

Published by

The Haworth Pastoral Press®, an imprint of The Haworth Press, 10 Alice Street, Binghamton, NY
13904-1580.

PUBLISHER'S NOTE
The development, preparation, and publication of this work has been undertaken with great care.
However, the Publisher, employees, editors, and agents of The Haworth Press are not responsible
for any errors contained herein or for consequences that may ensue from use of materials or
information contained in this work. The Haworth Press is committed to the dissemination of ideas
and information according to the highest standards of intellectual freedom and the free exchange of
ideas. Statements made and opinions expressed in this publication do not necessarily reflect the
views of the Publisher, Directors, management, or staff of The Haworth Press, Inc., or an
endorsement by them.

Identities and circumstances of individuals discussed in this book have been changed to protect
confidentiality.

Cover design by Marylouise E. Doyle.

Library of Congress Cataloging-in-Publication Data

Brister, C. W.
 Spiritual wisdom for successful retirement : living forward / C. W. Brister.
  p. cm.
 Includes bibliographical references and index.
 ISBN-13: 978-0-7890-2803-7 (hc. : alk. paper)
 ISBN-10: 0-7890-2803-4 (hc. : alk. paper)
 ISBN-13: 978-0-7890-2804-4 (pbk. : alk. paper)
 ISBN-10: 0-7890-2804-2 (pbk. : alk. paper)
 1. Retirees—Religious life. 2. Retirement—Religious aspects—Christianity. 3. Retirement—
Religious aspects. I. Title.

BV4596.R47B75 2006
248.8'5—dc22
                                                                          2006002581

To
Nathan Larry Baker

CONTENTS

ABOUT THE AUTHOR

C. W. Brister, PhD, is an author, international lecturer, and professional counselor who has been a theological educator for over forty years. He formerly held the Warren Hultgren Chair of Pastoral Care at Southwestern Baptist Theological Seminary in Fort Worth, Texas, where he also served as Distinguished Professor of Pastoral Ministry.

Acknowledgments

As the dedication page indicates, this book honors Nathan Larry Baker, a dear friend for more than half a century. Our relationship embraces multiple ties: I as his teacher in theological school; later, we served as ministering colleagues in varied settings; and he has been my confidant in sharing conversations through the years. Because Larry is a gifted observer of human nature and events—both religious and secular—I have trusted his judgment and profited from his wisdom.

Anticipating retirement after forty-five years of service as a theological educator, I was asked to deliver the Founders Day address at our alma mater. I titled the address: "Fifty Years of Pastoral Education at Southwestern Seminary: Looking Back and Living Forward." In discussing a possible title for this volume, Baker suggested *Living Forward* (now the subtitle) from that address as most appropriate. I am indebted to Larry and his life companion, Wanda, for their comradeship in the faith represented here. They both read this manuscript in an earlier stage and assisted with valuable comments. Because of their fundamental integrity and caring concern, the Bakers are a strengthening life force for my wife, Gloria, and myself.

The specific idea for writing a book on spiritual wisdom for retirement living arose during preparation of a previous manuscript, *Change Happens: Finding Your Way Through Life's Transitions*. Few transitions in life require such multifaceted, compelling, and time-sensitive decisions as those involved in the process of planning for and living in retirement. In putting forth my best wisdom about what it takes to retire with a measure of success, I feel a kinship with Alfred, Lord Tennyson's lines from *Ulysses*.

> I am a part of all that I have met.
> Yet all experience is an arch where-thro'
> Gleams that untravell'd world, whose margin fades
> Forever and forever when I move.

Spiritual Wisdom for Successful Retirement
Published by The Haworth Press, Inc. 2006. All rights reserved.
doi:10.1300/5537_a

Garnering many friendships across time and over the world is one of the privileges of growing older. In this endeavor, beyond the Bakers, I am grateful for the assistance of Drs. Nancy Ellett Allison, David L. Petty, William M. Pratt, and Derrel R. Watkins, each of whom read an early version of the book and responded with care. Allison serves as a minister in Charlotte, North Carolina. Petty is a retired gerontologist, educator, and author in New Mexico. Bill Pratt retired from a successful career as a minister/psychologist in Houston, and Watkins is a distinguished educator, editor, and author in his own right.

This book has been written with the computer resources provided as a gift from our son, Mark A. Brister, currently president of Oklahoma Baptist University. My wife, Gloria, is due a great measure of gratitude for her steadfast friendship, giftedness, support, and understanding. A special debt of gratitude is due to Jeffrey Bit Fai Kwok, who assisted with technical preparation of the final manuscript in hard copy and compact diskette format. A Hong Kong native, Dr. Kwok and his wife, Ring, anticipate careers as Christian educators. For each of my family members and friends I am profoundly grateful.

Introduction

"Once Before I Die" is the story of seven amateur mountaineers who climbed Koh-i-Tundy, a 20,000-foot peak in the Hindu Kush mountains of Afghanistan, filmed by Michael Wadleigh for the NBC Television Network. I have long been intrigued by the fantasies embraced in that memorable phrase. The life direction of those adventurers pointed toward the future rather than the past. The mountain climbers realized nostalgia is not a strategy for achieving life's goals. Their determination epitomizes this book's theme of *Living Forward*.

Wise seniors sense the universal human longing for getting all the way through with life, achieving everything we'd hoped for—"once before we die." There may be the goal of wisely planned financial security or of seeing our children married and firmly established in their careers. A fabled travel site—like Machu Picchu, the lost Incan city in Peru's Andes mountains; or Agra, India's famed Taj Mahal, or a cruise on the mystic Li River in Guilin, China—may hold fascination for you. We'd like to do "this or that"—visit an old friend in a far-off city, study art, or attend university commencement exercises for our youngest grandchild before we exit Planet Earth.

LIFE ON THE JOURNEY

Life is like that, not just awareness of the physical evidences of aging, but the inner longing to reach long-cherished goals. Along the way, we want to know how to stay fit and to live well. We covet physical strength, freedom from debilitating illness, and emotional passion to finish the course well. In our "spin"-saturated world, we hunger for matters of substance, abiding joy, and relational connections grounded in eternal values.

During postdoctoral study of psychiatry in a major medical school, I was reminded clinically of what I already believed theologically—that we are unitary beings. The human self is body, mind, and spirit.

Spiritual Wisdom for Successful Retirement
Published by The Haworth Press, Inc. 2006. All rights reserved.
doi:10.1300/5537_01

The Greeks called a person *anthropos*—"the upward-looking one." Humankind is incurably religious, fashioned for eternity. Historically, personal belief systems about God or a Higher Power have been incorporated into the institutions and worship practices of human communities. World religions—whether Judeo-Christian, Islamic, Hindu, or Buddhist—offer adherents a path toward eternity and rituals for the practice of worship. Because we are created spiritual beings, life's pilgrimage points to our true home in the heart of our Creator. Still, we need wisdom to avoid pitfalls and to follow the high road to our ultimate destination in eternity.

SPIRITUAL WISDOM

A book pledging *spiritual wisdom* proposes more than an "in-word." It recognizes *spirit* or *soul* as the essence of being human, implanted originally by the Creator (Gen. 2:7, NIV). Today, researchers report renewed attention is being given to faith factors in human experience. Religious indicators point to an upsurge of interest in life's basic meaning and values.[1] Since 9/11, terrorist threats have heightened concern about life's purpose, personal safety, and essential differences among adherents of various world religions.

The mention of *spirituality* inspires both scholarly interest and personal devotion. Despite the impressions of some thinkers that "the quest for the true . . . meaning of spirituality is a fool's errand," spiritual concerns are vital to life, identity, community, and holistic well-being.[2] Research findings reveal strong support for what Paul Tillich, a half-century ago, called the "ultimate concern" of existence. Today, 96 percent of Americans believe in God; 71 percent profess belief in some kind of afterlife; and 90 percent regularly pray.[3] There is a serious ethics gap, however, between the faith people affirm and their lifestyles. "Religion is highly popular in this country, but survey evidence suggests that it does not change people's lives to the degree one would expect from the level of professed faith."[4]

To speak of "spiritual wisdom" implies ultimacy and anchorage in life's original Source. Spirituality links humankind to the Creator, with a unique set of boundaries, values, and laws for living. Through creation, the human family is linked to all of life—to nature, history, culture, and the cosmos. Spirituality's goal is to certify one's commitment to God and stewardship of all life. Our spiritual nature fosters a search for meaning, a desire for inner wholeness, a craving for companionship, and a sense of accountability with and for all "the others." In addition, medical researchers report the value of faith factors for reducing anxiety, increasing hope, and providing a sense of control over life's variable risks and unavoidable changes.[5]

How can spiritual wisdom, viewed thus, foster successful retirement? As we age, life tumbles in upon us with a thousand serendipities—gifts, crises, hopes, fears, limitations, joys, and possibilities. Retired persons struggle to deal with real and symbolic losses as they redefine their identities, face uncertain financial futures, adapt to altered living arrangements, and become more aware of physical limitations. The future seldom unfolds precisely the way we plan. Disappointments, adversities, and suffering open us to the spiritual domain. Indeed, life needs a shepherd—a transcendent Guide on the journey.

Not only do seniors want to live healthily and productively into the future, they desire what the ancient Greeks called *sophia* (wisdom) for the journey. This book's title is *Spiritual Wisdom for Successful Retirement.* "How does a person become wise?" you may ask. Is it by experiencing failures to act wisely—by violating one's core values, overlooking lessons from history, failing in human relationships, wasting one's resources, or accumulating deficits of the human spirit? Ancient Israel's story related in the Hebrew scriptures offers another perspective on how to gain wisdom. Although not always faithful, the Jews were told that true wisdom is expressed by obeying God in all things.

Being true to my own faith heritage, I believe the Holy Scriptures offer guidance for retirees facing today's complex and pressing issues. The Bible presents God as the Creator of all that exists and the Caller of each person to his or her true vocation. Beyond employment in a particular occupation, a divine summons to one's vocation—from the Latin *vocatio*—is a call to surrender to God's eternal purpose. Obeying that divine design, through the instruction of the Holy Spirit, permits us to engage in a lifelong vocation through the "high calling of God." Self-surrender is the path to true selfhood.

WE ARE NOT ALONE

We are not alone on the road to retirement. The number of people age sixty-five and older more than tripled over the past half-century to a record 420 million worldwide. In general, seniors are better educated, retiring earlier, and living longer—in a period called by some observers "the third stage of life." Think of the differences in quality of life between retired persons living in developed nations, such as the United States and Japan, and those in developing countries, such as Colombia, Malaysia, Zimbabwe, and Costa Rica.

The U.S. Census Bureau predicts that by 2050 this nation's population will almost double to 450 million. Today, Anglos form 69 percent of the U.S. population. That proportion will shrink to 50 percent by 2050 through immigration and birth rates of Hispanics, Asians, and African Americans. Such findings raise important public policy questions for the coming decades. Can countries provide adequate health care? What kind of pension and retirement systems can retirees expect? Baby boomers, now working, may find they must rely on their own savings and investments for retirement to an even greater extent than do present-day seniors.

With issues like these in mind, retirees and their caregivers are invited to join me on the journey to "retirementland." Not all of the topics explored here will fit every reader's needs. Individuals who live and work among retirees know how suddenly life's events can plunge persons and families into situational and spiritual chaos. Challenging retirees' growing edges and intervening in their struggles, losses, illnesses, and decisions requires patience, physical and emotional energy, and wise understanding. Persons facing or experiencing retirement can benefit from the support of family members, caring friends and congregations, public agencies, as well as from their personal faith.

In looking at the whole picture, wise caregivers will explore a retiree's unique context, support system, and spiritual resources. Sharing journeys of faith by both retirees and their sojourners is characterized by mystery and by the recognition that any life design, this side of eternity, is proximate, not complete. We live with the promise that persons who persevere "will receive the crown of life that God has promised to those who love him" (James 1:12, NIV).

Chapter 1

A Funny Thing Happened
on the Way to Retirement

You may have read veteran reporter Tom Brokaw's *The Greatest Generation* in which he chronicled personal stories of veterans who lived through the tumultuous events of World War II. Today, many of those men and women have retired or died.[1] As they came home and started families, however, they gave birth to another unique generation called the *baby boomers*. Now, many of those estimated 76 million Americans have become eligible for retirement.

The word *retire* may be used in various ways: from leaving office or employment to retreating from public life; from involuntary termination of a job, to completing a hitch in military service, to withdrawing into oneself and becoming reclusive and unsociable. We, in Western cultures, assume a *retiree* is a person who has stopped working and has given up remunerated employment. I use the term with the latter meaning.

Today, the term *retirement* is worn like a loose-fitting garment. Many retired persons are not, technically, "retired." They are works-in-progress, waiting for their next assignment. Healthy persons who exit a job or leave the military generally refuse to retire from the world. They cling to life, to connections with family and friends, and they seek to remain engaged. They do not stop living but come to terms with a new season of existence.

Fellow trekkers can teach us much on the journey to retirement. Some employed persons have what a psychologist friend once described as "retirement fantasies." He and I caught a few minutes to chat privately between workshop sessions in Lake Tahoe. I mentioned that, although I had delayed the big "R," retirement was blipping on my radar screen. "It bothers me," I said, "that Western culture

Spiritual Wisdom for Successful Retirement
Published by The Haworth Press, Inc. 2006. All rights reserved.
doi:10.1300/5537_02

defines a person by what the individual *does,* instead of who he or she *is.* I'm still puzzling over the question of 'who am I when I'm not working?'"

His response was picturesque and compelling. "Some men have sexual fantasies, but I have retirement fantasies. True, I lead conferences all over the world, meet lots of interesting people. But I look forward to the day when I can stop running to the airport, hopping on a plane, and keeping my next appointment. My idea of *real living* is being on the trail, wilderness hiking, or mountain climbing." Meanwhile, his date book is filled with future engagements.

His confession, along with the substance of his presentations, led me to wonder about his life goals and ultimate values. "You've used the term *spiritual* several times during these days," I observed. "How does your view of spirituality influence you?"

Guided more by his scientific orientation than by religious belief, his reply was cryptic: "Spirituality is a link to a higher power. For me, that power is nature."

Our visit reminded me of Martin Luther King Jr.'s observation: "The means by which we live have outdistanced the ends for which we live. Our scientific power has outrun our spiritual power. We have guided missiles and misguided men." Whether a salaried employee or retired, a person must possess a reason to live. You may be trying to fit pieces of the retirement puzzle into a meaningful pattern for yourself.

PIECES OF THE RETIREMENT PUZZLE

People in various nations of the world view retirement differently—from the wealthy, thirty-something athlete who "retires" from playing the game to the impoverished Laotian rice farmer who will likely work until he drops dead or is taken out by some fatal accident or illness. Persons who entered a branch of the armed forces as adolescents or young adults may retire in midadulthood, free to pursue any number of options. They can return to school and complete a college degree or pursue a new area of inquiry. Younger retirees may re-enter the labor force, purchase a business, play golf, roam the world's vacation hot spots, or buy a tract of land and raise cattle. Many military jet pilots, trained at government expense, become commercial airline pilots following completion of their tour of duty. The same is true of medical and dental personnel who fulfill their military service obligations in order to repay tuition paid for an expensive education. Few of them remain in the military as an occupation, preferring relocation into private or group practice instead.

Retirement for many women is merely an interlude during child-bearing and early child-rearing years. They are often eager to reenter the workforce—from teaching to nursing, from computers to communication, from medicine to law—in order to enhance their feelings of personal worth, contribute to society, or ensure their financial security.

The truth is, retirees seldom "retire" completely from active life. They keep on keeping on. Jim, for example, is a fifty-nine-year-old contractor. He and his crew construct concrete foundations, driveways, patios, sidewalks, and steps for new houses. He was slowed down ten years ago with an angina attack, requiring stent implantation. That started him thinking about medical retirement. Recently, Jim had triple bypass heart surgery—another wake-up call. As a financial measure, he and his son pooled their resources some years ago and purchased farm property in order to raise cattle. Because he may not always be able to manage the construction game, marketing cattle generates income without requiring too much physical exertion. Clearly, Jim has no intention of retiring. He enjoys fishing and golfing as leisure hobbies and is in love with life.

Consider a different story. A public speaker related key life events, most of which were tied to her husband's career. Speaking to older, affluent women at a social club luncheon, she told of her husband's employment as the chief executive officer of a major aircraft production company. He retired when the firm was purchased by a new group of investors. In a quick turnaround, he was recalled as a consultant by the new company owners; thus, he gave up early retirement. In time, he was appointed to a high-ranking government office by a new administration in the nation's capitol. "When he retires for the third time," she said smiling, "I hope he actually means it." Interestingly, vocational research reveals that the average American male will be employed in at least seven different occupations over a career lifetime.

We discover when reading the *Scottsdale* (Arizona) *Journal* that many elderly retirees enjoy dancing in the Phoenix area every night. They are not alone, as many surveys have shown, wrote Peter

Kilborn. "Romance and lovemaking thrive among about half of Americans in their 60's and beyond."[2] How do they get together, you may ask? Contacts are initiated by dating services and "Seniors Seeking Seniors" personal newspaper advertisements, along with the community grapevine, friends, and the desire to thrive beyond retirement. Most seniors are not content to live in nursing homes, viewed euphemistically as "geriatric playpens." They gravitate to nature's warm spots—Orlando and Naples, Florida; Phoenix and Sun City, Arizona—determined to live to the brim all that's left of life. They visit through Internet chat rooms, attend forums and church worship services, socialize while shopping or playing golf, or may be introduced by friends.

"We can still appreciate a nice bod," said Joan Shafer, the widowed, seventy-five-year-old mayor of Surprise, a fast-growing town northwest of Phoenix. "Just because we are the age we are, it doesn't mean we don't have fantasies." Mary Ann, for example, had long admired widowed Judd Harrington, a village postmaster. She arranged, through a friend, to meet Judd by attending his church's worship services. Their "chance meeting" was far from accidental and sparked a rewarding relationship. In time, they joined other couples for meals, entertainment events, and extended travel experiences. While remaining single, they functioned as a couple and transcended loneliness with an enriching friendship.

Deann, a widow for more than twenty years, reflected on her numerous opportunities for dating and remarriage. "Unfortunately," she demurred, "most of the men I met were looking either for a nurse or a purse." Today, that seventy-something former single is enjoying a happy second marriage.

A major hitch in postretirement matchmaking, however, is the shortage of healthy, able-bodied men. The 2000 U.S. Census found 20.6 million women and 14.4 million men sixty-five and older, or ten women for every seven men. In Sun City, near Phoenix, "the median age is 75, and there are three times more widowed and divorced women than unattached men."[3] Furthermore, remarriage is fraught with complications, such as eventual inheritances for children and risks to pensions and alimony for widows and divorcees.

Loneliness is a shadow side to the retirement puzzle. Visiting an eighty-six-year-old widowed friend recently, I was reminded of the courage and determination it takes for some retirees to live. Like 95 percent of senior Americans, she has chosen to live at home rather than in a care center or assisted-living facility. A cancer survivor, she has numerous health anomalies, depends on a part-time housekeeper to prepare her meals, and relies on friends to assist with errands and trips to her numerous physicians. Although plagued with health problems, Edith trusts in God and stays connected with her out-of-state children by phone.

Add to that the experience of many elders who, because of lack of visual acuity—caused by macular degeneration, age, or infirmity—lose their legal driving privileges. Giving up driving for oneself forces many seniors into a dependant state they would never have freely chosen. In addition to this grief, time spent in waiting for a ride—whether a retirement center–provided van, family member, or personal friend—may drag painfully from minutes into hours. A visit with one such woman led her to observe, "Thanks for coming to see me. You have put me in touch with the world again."

Caregivers are aware of the human urge to stay involved, to remain connected to the human community as long as humanly possible. When teased about his travels to conferences and professional workshops, an eighty-one-year-old retired educator's stock reply was: "Out of sight—out of mind." Frank was determined not to ride off into the sunset, unacknowledged and unappreciated. What should we learn from such retirees? At the outset, we must discard the theory of disengagement.

"THEY KEEP CALLING ME BACK"

We had laid to rest the earthly frame of my wife's favorite cousin in an idyllic setting near some giant oak trees in a Louisiana cemetery. As many Southerners are disposed to do in such settings, we visited with the grieving relatives and bade them farewell before leaving for home. A funeral is often the only occasion for a family gathering until the "next time" someone dies. Such rituals run deep in some cultures.

Turning to leave, I spotted one of the funeral directors moving away from the burial site toward a vehicle owned by the funeral company. Going over to thank him for directing the graveside arrangements, I introduced myself.

"I know you," he said with a wry grin. "I'm Jack McRay, married to Marion Kern. Don't you remember me?"

"Yes, of course," came the spontaneous reply. "But it's been so long. I thought you had retired. Thanks for remembering me and for assisting so well with the service."

Then came his surprising reply. "I've retired thirty-two times. But they keep calling me back. I wasn't supposed to be here today, but one of the staff had an out-of-town emergency, so they asked me to help. They just keep calling me back; so, I help out when needed." I looked steadily into his warm, wrinkled face. "I'm eighty-two years old," he said. "Marion and I live in a retirement center near the airport."

We shook hands and then parted, but his having retired thirty-two times caught my attention. Why would a person bid good-bye to his life's work, arrange to live in an upscale retirement community, anticipate his spouse's needs, make all the necessary financial plans to live without a salaried income, then step back into a job?

Negative thoughts emerged as possible solutions to my question. Did he need the money? Could he not stop working and find his worth in *being* rather than in *doing*? Was his sense of identity tied so closely to his occupation that he could only be a funeral director? Did McRay need to be needed as a gracious caregiver for people facing the many losses attending death? Was there no place or psychic space for him in their reduced living area at the retirement village? Was he a refugee from a conflicted marriage? Did he gain inner satisfaction by maintaining power over death—humankind's last mortal enemy?

There were positive thoughts as well. Here was a man steeped in the faith of his forebears, resoundingly Christian in his religious persuasion, who enjoyed aiding folks in distress. There was a strong work ethic in his family upbringing. A person's worth resided heavily in what he or she could do, produce, or earn. There was the possibility of boredom and the need to get himself off of his hands. Lonely days in a small apartment may have prompted memories of social settings, group events, and the pleasure of being with people. Above all, he needed what all retired persons crave—a purpose to live.

The McRay work syndrome may or may not fit your own experience. Millions of retirees are content to make the most of what life brings, quite apart from an earlier workplace. They enjoy the slower pace, without a demanding agenda, and are at peace—free from the heavy responsibilities of life in the fast lane. Here's a retired physician, however, who agrees to substitute for colleagues several days each month. There is no longer the office expense and accountability of maintaining a full practice, but the satisfaction of keeping his clinical fingers sharp and caring for ill patients. There is no staff to supervise, no payroll to meet, no insurance claims to file, no hospital protocols into which to fit. He merely sees patients as a guest practitioner in a colleague's medical office.

Here's an ex-engineer who spends his retirement days working in his garden, reading, and visiting with his spouse, but he finds pleasure in being called back to the plant where he had functioned so many years as a highly paid petroleum engineer. His skills are just the ones needed for a particular project. Thus, he works piecemeal, receives a stipend, then retires again. A lawyer friend, who had served an appointment as a federal judge, became bored at home alone while his young spouse remained employed, so he gained credentials as a conflict resolution mediator and reentered the workplace.

Here is a ninety-two-year-old attorney who shows up in his law office at 6:30 a.m. each morning. Attending to a limited practice and arranging care for his invalid wife are his primary links with life. Like biblical Moses of old, whose "eyes were not weak nor his strength gone," Sam Alcorn keeps on keeping on. Having considered persons whose health, job situations, and locations permitted them to continue working beyond normal retirement years, what may we learn from individuals in particular circumstances?

FACING RETIREMENT
IN PARTICULAR CIRCUMSTANCES

By now, you have observed that I am using the phrase "a funny thing happened . . ." in the sense of particularity, uniqueness, and non-traditional events quite apart from the customary circumstances and protocols of leaving one's employment. Persons involved in caring for retirees readily understand that a "one size fits all" intervention process fails to take life's serendipitous events, disruptions, price tags of neglect, and vulnerabilities to chance and change into account. Also, individual differences in culture, age, gender, ethnicity, education, emotional health, adaptive capacities, financial condition, physical well-being, working environment, and support community are factors determining when and how a person may manage retirement.

An industrial accident may require medical attention and premature retirement.

Charles Foster, a forty-eight-year-old long-haul truck driver, had made a good living with his own big rig. He had worked for the other fellow long enough to save and invest in his own Mack tractor. Charles leased his auto-hauling semi to an automobile transport company. He delivered imported vehicles from ports such as Houston and Los Angeles to automobile dealerships in various U.S. cities. Also, he loaded new vehicles at American automobile assembly plants and transported them to new-vehicle dealers. His stay-at-home spouse was well provided for; they enjoyed a good life.

Once at a dealer's, while breaking down chains locking vehicles into place and lowering the rear platform, a truck slipped and pinned Charles's body to the trailer frame. It severed his left arm above the elbow. Although he was rushed to a local hospital emergency room, the medical staff could not save the severed arm. His wife was notified and flew to be at his bedside. Charles was not the independent, strong, self-assured man who had driven away from home a few days earlier. She found a broken man, with sutures and bandages around the stump that remained of his arm.

Without sufficient medical insurance, the Fosters were thrown into a financial crisis. After being fitted with a prosthesis and long-term physical therapy, Charles was unable to remain commercially licensed as a big-rig transport driver. He faced vocational reeducation in a rehabilitation program, fought depression for months, and felt less than a man in matters ranging from dressing himself to making love with his understanding mate.

An elected officeholder may lose a bid for reelection and face forced retirement.

A county commissioner held office for three four-year terms. People respected Lloyd Gayer and counted on his response to calls for assistance to repair bridges, to tarmac gravel roads, or to have his crew trim overgrown shrubs along rural byways. Gayer overreached the privileges of his office, however, by privately purchasing worn road construction equipment for "pennies on the dollar" of actual value. Instead of placing used items up for bids at public auction, he privately purchased the county's used bulldozers and paving equipment for his own subcontracting business.

As word spread that his subcontracting firm was using former government-owned equipment, Gayer's popularity plummeted. It was not just the "courthouse crowd" that was upset with his deceit and presumption. There was widespread dismay and criticism. He was soundly defeated in the next election and "turned out to pasture." Although he had made many friends during his tenure in public office, that popular support faded. At fifty-eight,

Lloyd Gayer found himself forced into involuntary retirement. Four years would elapse before he became eligible for a reduced Social Security stipend. Facing community disfavor added insult to injury.

A final concert tour or final operatic appearance makes retirement a reality.

Well-known names in the entertainment industry sometimes fade from public view. Whether it is the death of a once-popular member of a performing group, another marriage with new family interests, or desire for freedom from the demands of public stage appearances—singers leave performance halls behind. The celebrated tenor Luciano Pavarotti announced his retirement from the concert stage following marriage and the birth of a child. Barbra Streisand, a superstar in every sense of the word—popular in motion pictures and heralded by audiences across the world—gave a stellar performance in her final concert some years ago. Her life now moves on less demanding pathways.

The age-plus-length of service formula works for many retirees.

Many government agencies, educational systems, and service organizations have developed formulas permitting retirement when a person breaks the age-plus-service "code." Nell's story describes such an achievement. Nell Courtney retired from an auditor's position with a state health department after reaching her twenty-five-year "age-plus-length of service" goal. Refusing to disengage, she now works part-time as a sales clerk for a national retail department store chain. "I enjoy being around other people," she explained.

Corporate downsizing forces many able employees into premature retirement.

Here, for example, is a communications major university graduate who was employed in the administrative ranks of a leading U.S. airline. Given developments in the low-budget domestic airline industry, rising fuel prices, the economic fallout following the World Trade Center terrorist attacks of 9/11, and renegotiated union contracts—from baggage handlers to veteran pilots—Arlene Sanders was "pink slipped." She had survived the upward movement of terminations until the company got to persons at her level of tenure and salary. As things would have it, her temporary "furlough" became a dismissal.

Arlene tried to reenter the airline communications field. Her former boss, now in Washington, DC, although pleased with her past job performance, had nothing to offer. After depleting her unemployment compensation income, she turned to her parents for temporary financial support. Arlene decided to upgrade her university degree to a master's level, but that became counter-productive. The involuntary retiree and her parents were pleasantly surprised when her social skills led to a serious dating relationship and, in time, to marriage. Now, reemployed on the West Coast, Arlene and her husband, Tom, are enjoying married life together.

Premature forced retirement often happens to the nicest people.

Involuntary retirement happens—whether one is in a high-tech industry, the business community, medical field, sports, government service, the travel business, education, construction, or sales—wherever money, sex, and power are dynamic factors. Such changes have consequences—like humiliation, economic hardship, enforced dependence (returning temporarily to one's parental home or moving in with a friend), resentment, occasional family violence, depression, re-tooling, just plain survival.

There are many reasons for forced change, such as corporate mergers, "right sizing," corporate scandals, outsourcing of production with plant closings, completing a tour of military duty, technology displacing paid jobs (even minimum-wage jobs like checkers at stores being replaced with self-check-out technology), devastation from natural disasters, crippling orthopedic accident, or critical illness such as some form of cancer, a heart attack, HIV infection, or AIDS. Many "mom and pop" enterprises wither under competition.

Hourly and daily workers—employees in the construction industry; service company staffers; and seasonal workers in income tax offices, lawn care businesses, theme parks, and tourism—may face irregular schedules and involuntary "retirements." Many such workers have minimal or no health insurance. Some unemployed persons become angry or depressed and engage in domestic violence and self-destructive behaviors. Migratory field workers do life from the "underside," experience separation from families, exist on subsistence wages, face frequent moves, live in crowded environments, and their school-age children must move from school to school. Financial security is only a figment of their imaginations or a hoped-for dream if they can break the cycle of poverty.

There are many ways to lose one's job—from napping at work to sending and receiving racy e-mail messages. Sudden termination usually triggers a period of forced retirement. In the event of sudden job loss, family members, social workers, medical, and other caring professionals will be sensitive to involuntary retirement's aftermath. Remain alert to warning signs of possible depression, alcohol or prescription drug abuse, evidence of domestic violence, and suicidal tendencies. Care providers will emphasize the need for a job searcher to stay open to hopeful possibilities as a new life evolves.

RETIREMENT IS A NEW LIFE

Retirees soon discover that retirement is more than one event. It is a new life, involving a process of decision making. Psychologist Nancy K. Schlossberg, a retiree herself, has described retirees' adaptation tasks in her book *Retire Smart, Retire Happy: Finding Your True Path in Life.*[4] Following interviews with current and prospective retirees, she developed a simple typology of various personality types, including Continuers, Adventurers, Searchers, Retreaters, and Easy Gliders. Schlossberg shows how understanding one's personality type can help a person use strengths and resources in the transition process. The former University of Maryland professor confessed that one of her reasons for writing the book was to work through issues she was dealing with herself.

A clue that a retired person may be in a crisis is evidenced when he or she feels overwhelmed by life's circumstances. A healthy retiree takes life's events in stride. When they have an anticipated specific cut-off date, many retirees plan well: deciding on the preferred area of the country in which to live; electing to stay in a present home or to relocate (perhaps into scaled down living arrangements); and considering financial resources (such as anticipated income streams and the preferred state's personal income tax requirements), nearness to family; reliable medical resources; a congenial worship fellowship; a support community; and opportunities for volunteer service, continuing education, airport access for travel, and availability of the arts and life enrichment programs.

"I've helped countless individuals deal with their stuff," acknowledged a veteran minister. "I've written books to help caregivers know how to deal with life's issues; but I've been helpless to help myself." Psychologist Michael Yapko has commented on such a predicament: "To be a victim means doing nothing to . . . change the circumstances on your own behalf." Viewing yourself as a victim "implies you are powerless to change either the circumstances if possible, or to change your reactions to the circumstances if they are truly unchangeable."[5]

Retirees who stay on top of things, who seek stimulating ways to live on the creative edge of their retirement years, know how to face reality. They do not imagine how things "should" be when they no longer have a workplace environment. They make a *place* at home for themselves before retiring, may enjoy a hobby, or volunteer for service with an altruistic motive. Here is a retiree, for example, who enjoys picture framing as a hobby. In relocating to a new residence, he set up part of his garage as a small woodworking shop, with storage space for tools and framing materials. He also volunteers as a financial consultant to an educational institution. He has experienced health problems, including knee replacement surgery, yet he and his wife are adapting nicely to their new realities.

My wife and I, along with a host of guests, recently heard Pulitzer Prize-winning author Frank McCourt, seventy-five, describe his life before and after retirement. An unnoticed teacher for thirty years in New York's public schools, in 1996, at age sixty-six, McCourt's memoir of a miserable Irish childhood, *Angela's Ashes* (Simon & Schuster, Inc., 1996), catapulted him into literary fame and fortune. Two best-selling memoirs have followed: *'Tis* (Scribner, 1999) and *Teacher Man* (Scribner, 2005). He's a literary superstar.

> I wasn't prepared for it. After teaching, I was getting all this attention. They actually looked at me—people I had known for years—and they were friendly and they looked at me in a different way. And I was thinking 'All those years I was a teacher, why didn't you look at me like that then?'[6]

Not everyone can expect to duplicate McCourt's success in seniorhood, but we can *be* all we were meant to be.

Rather than feeling victimized in retirement, these creative persons seized opportunities to alter their living arrangements, to contribute to the larger good, or to achieve a lifelong dream. Keep in mind that these retirees were not social isolationists but shared in "the living human web" of existence. Rather than ignoring what lay ahead, they took steps to address specific life issues or to pursue long-held dreams. The lesson in such stories is to take steps in a healthy direction that will yield positive results in your own retirement years. Following a brief summary, we shall explore life on the road to retirement.

A SUMMARY OF KEY POINTS

- Where do you fit in the American age spectrum—a preretiree or an elder? At the beginning, we distinguished persons whom

Tom Brokaw called "the greatest generation" from the emerging retirees of the baby boomer generation. Are you enrolled in "Retirement 101," planning for those freer years yourself? What are you considering about basic issues such as living arrangements, financial needs, health care, and mortality?

- Read again the story of Jack McRay ("I've retired thirty-two times.") How do you account for the fact that so many retirees remain engaged with life? Do you know should-be-retired persons who keep going on and on like the "Engergizer Bunny?" How do they stay connected with other people, continue to enjoy an extended family, reading, travel, art, or nature, and remain active in a faith community of their choice?

- Why do you suppose so many care providers neglect the needs of frail persons such as Edith, the eighty-six-year-old cancer survivor (see previous story)? Do elderly persons remind you of your own vulnerability to disease, deterioration, and death? How highly defended are you against the corrosives of time? Rather than withdrawing from members of the older generation, should caregivers listen attentively to elderly persons around them?

- Are you tempted to use a "one size fits all" approach to attending to the needs of retired persons? Are they experiencing a push/ pull-click/click brush-off from you instead of your attending to, hearing, and understanding their stories? How do factors such as individual differences of age, gender, ethnicity, culture, education, adaptive capacities, emotional well-being, financial status, physical health, and support community influence a person's adaptation to retirement living?

- Retired persons are part of a larger social system ("a living human web") that includes their family members, former employer(s), financial institutions, neighbors, faith community, medical resources, fellow citizens, and cultural context. Part of the caregiver's task is to encourage potential retirees to anticipate changes and plan well for their freer years. You can be their teacher, resource guide, and friend on the journey.

- Retired persons must deal with *multiple causality* issues. They may worry about health matters, experience surgery, then discover that insurance failed to cover costs involved in their particular procedure. (1) Health issues cause (2) financial concerns;

then, there are (3) transport for therapy concerns; (4) perhaps special equipment at home needs; and (5) nursing care needs. One event leads to another. You may not be able to do everything for retirees in your care. As a ministry manager, you can mobilize and train volunteers to assist with elder-care issues in your particular setting.

- Focus on health, wellness, and positive features with elders in your faith community, not simply problems and crises. You are more than a situational firefighter—putting out emergency blazes. You are a spiritual mentor; thus, you represent divine as well as human resources. It is a high calling to help retirees maintain their dignity and independence and to pray for and encourage their family members and care providers on the journey of faith.

Chapter 2

The Road to Retirement

Persons who have given up employment discover many avenues, not just one path, on the road to retirement. Retirement is both a point on life's journey and a process, ending only at one's death. Leaving employment is usually an anticipated event or series of events, but it can happen in an unplanned, chaotic manner, through accidents, adversities, and historic changes. My wife and I have a friend, for example, who invited us, months in advance, to her "big" retirement dinner at an exclusive club. It was designed for business and civic leaders in the city. She also asked us to come to an office-type venue, scheduled later, for a colleague-related event. Planning ahead, she had already agreed to serve on a number of organizational boards and pledged to work part-time as a consultant with her professional group.

Experiences of a different sort happen to individuals who lose their positions when organizational leadership changes or some critical event occurs. Changes from corporate scandals, corporate takeovers, sell-offs, or mergers; downsizing; bankruptcy; decline in sales or in market share; outsourcing of products; and reversals in the workplace environment force many Americans to retire without a clear future path. Completing an anticipated hitch in a branch of military service may provide a veteran a smooth transition into a new vocation, but to have been wounded in battle, injured in an accident, or failed to achieve the next upgrade may lead to an unplanned retirement.

Self-employed persons, without the benefits of an automatic 401(k) savings plan, must also pay for their own health care insurance and Social Security benefits. Their occupations may have differed from accounting to dairy farming, but their future needs and risks have similarities. Retiring at sixty-five may leave twenty to thirty years of postretirement living ahead. For example, I visited with an eighty-one-year-old salesman who regrettably realized he had retired

Spiritual Wisdom for Successful Retirement
Published by The Haworth Press, Inc. 2006. All rights reserved.
doi:10.1300/5537_03

too soon. "Are you working for fun or because you have to?" He frowned with the reply: "I'm working because I have to work."

The road to retirement requires information, goal setting, imagination, realistic planning, and flexibility. The longer the planning horizon, the wiser one's preparation can be—from living arrangements to financial matters—from farewells in the workplace to new beginnings, perhaps with new surroundings. Planning should include a whole range of variables, not financial matters alone. The following personal reflection may help preretirees and their caregivers rethink the changes one may face in becoming a retiree. It is a lesson from nature.

AS THE RIVER FLOWS

Native Americans have reminded us that the first roads on this continent were rivers. I have crossed the Trinity River thousands of times in more than a half-century of living in north central Texas. Viewing the Trinity from a new perspective, in moments of reflection, I saw the stream in a new light. I was standing by a large window, on the fifteenth floor of Fort Worth's City Center Tower II, when I observed the river's West Fork, flowing from Eagle Mountain Lake, merging with the Clear Fork, flowing from Lake Benbrook. The two streams became one—the West Fork of the Trinity—flowing toward a bend in the river. There was no way to envision its direction beyond the bend, save that maps show it twisting in an easterly direction toward Dallas, then merging with the East Fork of the river. I was reminded of the *unknowns* when facing impending retirement.

The Trinity River begins unimpressively in Archer County, Texas; explodes in torrents during great rains; is held in catchments like Lake Bridgeport, Eagle Mountain Lake, and Lake Worth; then flows hundreds of miles into the Gulf of Mexico. *It was that elusive bend in the river that pricked my imagination.* What course would its flow actually take, because most rivers flow to the sea? Like a retiree's uncertain identity and adaptive tasks ahead, it was the river's mysterious course that intrigued me.

According to one observer's biblical worldview, "a personal revelation through particular circumstances of time and space is the only way to become acquainted with the [Hebrew-Christian understanding of] God and his purposes."[1] Nature alone does not hold ultimate meaning, but it can point to such meaning. Thus, I wondered, given reflection, what the bend in the river was revealing. Its message melded with Jesus' words in the ancient apostle John's vision: "I am making everything new!" (Rev. 21:4b-5, NIV). Facing retirement's challenges is like kayaking in white-water rapids. Spiritual wisdom in such circumstances requires careful thought, vision, and passion for what lies ahead.

What are some lessons from the bend in the river, inspired by reflections on God's power to make all things new? I discovered wisdom in the river's flow.

One, rivers flow in natural channels, form deep pools and dangerous shallows, bear the weight of great ships and small pleasure craft, endure floods, nurture fish and waterfowl, resource recreation, and quench the thirst of a land and its people. Forests, fields, and flowers are nourished by the world's rivers. Although a river appears to follow the course of least resistance, it actually follows its ancient channel to the sea. Spring fed, a river is everflowing, subject to pollution, yet intentional—blending with other streams seaward. So, life for retired persons refuses to follow the path of least resistance and seeks wise, dependable counsel.

Two, the world's great rivers give themselves away naturally to provide access to continents and life to the inhabitants of a land. Just so, a retiree is to remain engaged in order to share the spiritual, physical, and emotional well-being of one's family and the larger community. What a person spent a lifetime learning, achieving, and accruing must not be wasted on incidentals but rather invested in matters of consequence. In planning for retirement, a person must refuse some things in order to maximize resources and energy for those most needful and worthwhile enterprises.

Three, Pierre Teilhard de Chardin inspired a third lesson from his treatise on happiness. Following the river analogy, a truly happy life in the time remaining will add its tributary to the *main* channel. One may elect to volunteer for some worthwhile cause, craft a patterned quilt, write a book, draft an architectural design, pursue medical research, compose music, prepare a life review, or advocate a passionate cause. Seniors need not try to "beat their own track record" by doing something out of the ordinary. I know of older persons who have adopted extravagant, risky hobbies, such as skydiving, deep sea scuba diving, speeding on a Harley-Davidson, drag racing, or sailing alone for long distances in dangerous waters. A retired person's ambitions need not overshadow a lifetime of valuable accomplishments.

Teilhard de Chardin wrote: "We must add one stitch, no matter how small it be, to the magnificent tapestry of life."[2] A person who cares deeply about life will add his or her energies to the marvelous currents of existence. At the end of the day, one's life will flow into that immortal sea of God's ultimate love, provision, and care.

Four, a river is content to be itself—sometimes placid, at other times a wild thing. Some streams are shallow, others deep. Some, like the Mississippi River, define a continent; others are short, narrow, and small. Some waterways are clear and sparkling, spring fed and cold; others are murky, polluted, and silt-laden. A river is never in conflict with itself. Its purpose is to flow, despite hindrances, on its circuitous route to the sea.

What is the river's message to persons leaving the nine-to-five life? You may need to alter your perception of retirement. Many retirees would like to erase *retirement* from the dictionary, because they resent the implication that they are giving up or being pushed aside. In contrast, some people regard retirement as being set free after all those years.

Five, rivers receive as well as give. Cartographers note, for example, that some 200 tributaries feed into South America's Amazon River. The late Henri J. M. Nouwen noted that receiving is often harder than giving. Giving is important: giving insight, giving hope, giving courage, giving advice, giving support, giving money, and, most of all, giving ourselves. Without giving, there is no real community. Receiving is just as important, however, because by receiving we reveal to the givers that they have gifts to offer. When we say, "Thank you, you gave me hope; thank you, you gave me a reason to live; thank you, you allowed me to realize my dream," we make givers aware of their unique and precious gifts. Sometimes it is only in the eyes of the receiver that givers discover their gifts.[3]

Reflecting on the Trinity River flowing toward the Gulf of Mexico was illuminating as I anticipated my own retirement. Like a river nourished by mountain springs and melting snows, I recognized the true Source of my existence. Little did I know some of the surprising events—occasions of both joy and sorrow—that awaited me. With an altruistic outlook, healthy retirees trust that their latter years will supply lessons from reflections on experience and pass wisdom on to generations following.

Retirement is not as easy as one might imagine. It takes long-range planning and introspection to ensure that your work-free years are worry-free years. Here are some basic considerations when planning for the road ahead.

CHECK OUT YOUR LEGAL RETIREE BENEFITS

Your employer—whatever the entity or institution—likely has an employee's manual of policies, including terms for involuntary termination and well-earned retirement. I referred frequently to our school's faculty manual when anticipating departure from the ranks of the employed. The school's trustee board had adopted policies to encourage each faculty member's fullest expression of calling and ministry. Two important caveats! (1) The policies were subject to change in response to changing federal law, historic events, and available resources. (2) A retiree's Retirement Benefit Funding Amount (RBFA) would depend on a length of service formula, not merely employment at the institution.

Preretirement planning was encouraged, with options varying from full retirement, to salary reduction with a reduced teaching program, to retiring with the privilege of adjunctive teaching assignments based on instructional needs and policies at the time of retirement. Encouragement to gain and maintain financial security was uppermost in the guidelines. Preretirees were taught to plan so that retirement income—whether from social security, an annuity, spousal earnings, investments, individual retirement accounts, or personal savings—would be sufficient to cover anticipated expenses. All employees were informed about which benefits ceased when employment ended and which privileges continued into retirement.

Self-employed persons face a different set of circumstances from individuals leaving military, company, or institutional employment. Cost factors such as private medical, dental, and long-term care insurance must be assumed by the individual. Hourly workers, migrant workers, and day laborers must cope with entirely different futures. There are few, if any, employee benefits, like health care insurance, available in such cases. Many immigrants—legal or illegal—have only family support as they face seniorhood's potentially lean years. Money matters are addressed in greater detail in a later chapter.

A RATIONALE FOR RETIREMENT

Preretirement planners suggest that individuals have a formal, written plan as they anticipate the future. You cannot afford the luxury of experiencing retirement without thinking ahead. "If you haven't quantified what you want, then you have a dream rather than a goal," noted Stephen Leimberg, author of *Tools and Techniques of Employee Benefit and Retirement Planning*. Fail to plan well "and those dreams can become a nightmare."[4]

Sage wisdom from the Hallmark Card Co. of Kansas City spoke to me one Easter Sunday, a year before submitting a retirement letter to the school administration.

> As your retirement begins, choose your destinations well,
>   but do not hurry there.
> Avoid the shortcuts . . . wander the back roads . . . enjoy the
>   scenery along the way.
> And remember that the true worth of your travels lies not
>   in reaching a destination but
> in who you come to be along the way.

First, retirees should be convinced they have worth because they are created in the divine image, not because of paid employment. The theology of John Calvin, coupled with the Puritan work ethic, ingrains the notion that a responsible person produces, earns, and invests in order to generate "wealth." Not only that. In the pragmatic West, a job title shapes one's identity. A chemist does experiments. A physician heals or performs surgery. A carpenter builds things. A plumber plumbs for water use and sewerage disposal in buildings. A computer programmer creates Web sites, and so on. Retirement affects one's sense of identity. The big question becomes: "Who are you when you are not working?"

Once he had received my letter of intended retirement, the institution's president queried: "Are you as old as Dr. So-and-So?" When I replied affirmatively, he further asked: "What are you going to *do?*" He emphasized the *doing* part. He appeared stunned when I cryptically replied: "I am going to *be*, not do. This is a redirection for me, not just retirement." Contrary to some of my retired colleagues' actions, I had decided the academic environment would not be my only link with life.

Second, try wording your retirement notice well in advance of your formal departure. In my case, a pilot retirement letter to our administration was prepared two and a half years before I left employment. That tentative letter is still in my files. In wording the document, I tried to enter, imaginatively, into America's "formerly employed" ranks. Although I was in excellent health and busy with too many assignments—from directing the services of a special Center, to offering doctoral seminars, to chairing the institution's Financial Resources Committee, to sharing a self-study committee's tasks—change seemed wise. My seventieth birthday was history, and the academic environment was not fun anymore.

Third, a confluence of events—not a single cause—usually prompts a person to consider the Big Change. Age itself often forces the decision. Events formed a preretirement pattern in my own case. Our public relations staff asked that I prepare a fifty-year history of my academic department for publication. A faculty committee invited me to address our annual Founder's Day student chapel on a similar theme. Those assignments required careful research and thoughtful reflection. In that same time frame, several notable achievements pointed toward closure of my active employment. Events signaling a person's departure from public work are highly individualistic and contextual, but they are usually reliable indicators of transitions ahead.

Retiring in my experience became a win/win situation—personally and professionally. It was time for a change. Notes from my planning rationale read: "Upon honest reflection, not one, but a constellation of factors prompts my retirement. I have no job to go to—no [fantasy] plan—only a sense of obeying God into a redirected future. I need time with my wife, time to wait upon the Lord, time to write, time to travel, [yes] time to play. Change happens. Transitions occur. I need some distance from the academic environment [and] freedom . . . to enjoy the future God may be pleased to grant to both Gloria and me." Varied circumstances must be considered on the road to retirement.

CIRCUMSTANCES DETERMINE OUTCOMES

The levels of a retired person's adaptation, total wellness, and feelings of satisfaction are bound into the bundle of particular circumstances. Let us consider three experiences.

Identification May Hold Secondary Gain

Sue

One of the clearest evidences of satisfaction with one's retired status is the capacity to identify with the achievements of one's direct descendents and close relatives. Here is a single retiree from a large petrochemical company who stayed in close touch with her nieces. Sue followed their accomplishments during their high school and university years, identifying with one niece who was an outstanding soccer player and another who was in honors classes. Although she had the responsibility of caring for her frail elderly mother at home, Sue arranged visits with her "girls," as she called them. Their friends became her "friends." Their social calendars provided her opportunities to give them clothes, jewelry, and accessories for the big events. She was retired, with limited social outlets, but Sue gained satisfaction through Frances's and Ellen's achievements.

Ms. Redd

Grandparenthood often opens the door to identify with one or more favorite grandchildren, celebrate their special days, and share their successes and failures. Here is a widow, for example, whose husband was graduated from the University of Notre Dame. Although she enjoyed reports of all six grandchildren's achievements, Ms. Redd was bonded especially to grandson Russell. He had floundered a bit after completing university—working for a fast-food shop near the campus. Then his career took off!

Russ decided to move to New England and enroll in a specialized chef's school. A vegetarian himself, he had to learn to cook and enjoy eating a variety of foods. His closest friend moved to France where he influenced Russ to enroll in an advanced chef's training program. Ms. Redd described her great pleasure in the fact that, today, Russ works as the private chef for a Hollywood celebrity. His success, world travels, excellent salary, and social privileges on the West Coast have become "hers" as well. In fact, Ms. Redd's intergenerational satisfactions were the product of her ability to identify with and receive secondary gain from her grandson's well-placed achievements.

Sadly, a grandchild's life course can plummet into failure—such as chemical dependency, unplanned pregnancy, a tragic accident, or major illness. In such instances, grandparents are drawn into the economic and emotional mire of extended family matters.

The Immigrant Elderly

Chinese families are noted for their intergenerational linkage. There are millions of former residents of mainland China now living in such cities as Toronto, Sydney, Singapore, Auckland, Hong Kong, and Vancouver. Caregivers in America's metropolitan areas will notice large Chinese populations in cities like New York, Houston, Los Angeles, San Francisco, and Dallas. Once an Oriental family sends a son or daughter to America to attend university, it is anticipated that that young adult, once employed, will facilitate the immigration of relatives. Such extended family arrangements are more than ancestor worship; they are economic, physical, social, and moral lifestyles.

The Li family arranged for grandfather Wu to visit them in Texas. A retired businessman from the *new* China, where economics is a powerful engine in society and government, his initial visits were trial events. Eventually, he decided to leave his China factory in the hands of a trusted elder son and move to America with his daughter and her family. Their ways slowly became his ways—schedules, foods, television programs, newspapers (in Chinese for Mr. Wu), worship events, and holidays. One of the family's happiest moments came when their father committed himself to Christian beliefs and worship practices. In time, he received the ordinance of Christian baptism and accompanied his family to a Chinese-speaking congregation.

Money Matters

The level of comfort experienced by retired persons is largely determined by two factors: health and economics. Here, for example, is a Mexican family who has lived divided lives for several decades. Jose entered the United States illegally and worked as a ranch hand about forty years. He understood some English as a second language, but preferred to converse with the ranch owner in Spanish. He lived alone in a modest ranch cabin and sent money regularly to his wife and children in Mexico.

Jose's goal was, eventually, to bring his family into the United States. He had to get a green card and establish legal residence in his adopted country. Although his financial house was shaky, he brought his son to live with him on the ranch, to assist with the chores, and attend an American public school. Over the years, he managed to have each of his children follow that path. Late in life, he arranged for his wife to immigrate to the United States and live with relatives in a metropolitan Hispanic area. Now retirement age, Jose continues to split time between living on the ranch and visiting in the city with his wife's family.

Like millions of Mexican immigrants, the Martinez family lives at the edges of poverty and remains dependent on public health care and welfare.

The elders are closely identified with Hispanic language kindred, values, and practices; thus, they have never blended into the general U.S. population. Jose feels he will never retire. He works part-time and remains financially dependent on the generosity of his sponsoring ranch owner.

It was John Nash, the leading character in the book *A Beautiful Mind* and the movie with the same title, who said: "It is so difficult to have the architecture of your life pulled out from under you." The underpinnings of our lives are anchored by our core beliefs, vision, and values. The circumstances exemplified by the Li and Martinez families, although not exhaustive, illustrate the varieties of *givens* in human circumstances. People of upscale means retire to enjoy luxury cruises; inhabit condos in exotic resorts from Sun Valley, Idaho, to Florence, Italy; play golf with their fellow elite in well-maintained country clubs; travel on weekends to vacation spots as varied as Hawaii or Paris; and experience costly shopping events beyond the imaginations of ordinary retirees.

Anticipating retirement, my wife and I had built our dream home in a gated community. There was space for each of us to maintain our different centers of interest. As with many other retirees, we did the numbers to assess resources, determined our risk-tolerance levels with investments, and strove to attend to each other's needs for respect, health, safety, and financial security. Despite careful forethought we have encountered numerous forks in the road. Without divine guidance and intervention we and our extended family members may not have endured. Too many changes occur on the road to retirement to set things in stone. We continue to jettison old illusions that drew us to false goals and strive to follow the high road *home* to our Creator.

A SUMMARY OF KEY POINTS

- We have considered one person's philosophy of retirement living with the analogy of lessons from a river running to the sea. Specific tasks on the road to retirement were suggested, such as: (1) Read the fine print of your employer's retirement policies and provisions. (2) Write out an appropriate rationale and plan for your retirement years. (3) Consider and prepare for your lifestyle, but be alert to dislocations along the way.

- Preretirement planning was encouraged. Caregivers should suggest that persons anticipating retirement check the firm's vesting policies of their retirement funds. What employer contributions and employee matching funds are available in your retirement fund account? Are there long-term health care guarantees, privileges of using health club facilities (if any), and, for educators, the addition of *emeritus* to their identity title?
- When persons begin life mapping on the road to retirement, they will consider their particular circumstances that largely determine outcomes on the journey. Caregivers will both model and teach adaptive skills, suggest health care regimens, and refer retirees to proper resources to facilitate achieving life goals. Different kinds of considerations were illustrated—from elders identifying with younger family members, to extended family styles, to ethnic distinctions.
- In some respects, retirees are spiritual nomads searching for their "true home." Considering life's uncertainties will help caregivers work with real people facing real challenges. We now turn to matters such as financial planning, favorable locales for retirement living, health matters, leisure, computer skills, coping with the blahs and blues, and facing unplanned events and the certainty of death and the life beyond.

Chapter 3

Mapping the Retirement Landscape

Some years ago, my wife and I joined a favorite couple on a driving tour to Alaska. We had talked of such a trip during several previous vacation visits. At that time, our friends lived in a picturesque mountain village on Colorado's western slope, while we are from the flatlands of north central Texas. We calculated that such an extensive journey might take us nearly 10,000 miles. We elected to drive to Colorado, join them there, and then share driving tasks and expenses to Alaska. They had invested in a new van with a custom-made carrier installed on the roof rack to contain our luggage, foodstuffs, and other essential belongings.

Planning for the journey required us to agree on our major *objectives,* to set achievable *goals,* and to make good *decisions*—such as selecting the most favorable season for motoring across the Yukon Territory. Our principal objectives were to enjoy Alaska's vistas and people along the way, to visit Denali National Park, then to return by ferry on the Alaska Marine Highway—the famed Inland Passage. Months before departure, we attempted to reserve two shipboard cabins and ensure vehicle space on the ferry. That the only space available on our travel dates was a single cabin with four bunks provided the setting for close company and interesting events.

Mapping the agreed-on route was achieved by using the current edition of *The Alaska Milepost,* which detailed distances between cities on every major highway through Alberta, the Yukon, Northwest Territories, British Columbia, and Alaska.

Assessing the terrain and travel time required to drive between our daily destinations required joint decision making. Our Colorado friends volunteered to reserve overnight accommodations for the group. We agreed that flexibility in scheduling and facing the possibility of unexpected events was essential. Planning for that Alaska

Spiritual Wisdom for Successful Retirement
Published by The Haworth Press, Inc. 2006. All rights reserved.
doi:10.1300/5537_04

journey provides a paradigm for prospective retirees and would-be caregivers as they attempt to map the retirement landscape.

With the objective of successful retirement in mind, we shall first examine an appropriate framework for retiree care; then, we will consider responsibilities that potential retirees must assume (if at all possible) for themselves.

A FRAMEWORK FOR PROVIDING CARE

There are numerous models for viewing the human life cycle in relationship to aging and retirement. Each model reflects the significance of *temporality*—the fact that we are simultaneously immersed in the past, present, and future. Andrew Lester noted in *Hope in Pastoral Care and Counseling* that peoples' stories help them make sense out of life's ongoing events, which he describes with *narrative theory*.[1]

Charles Gerkin, late Professor of Pastoral Theology in Atlanta's Candler School of Theology, once proposed four models of Christian caregiving for retired persons and the elderly: a symmetrical model, a loss/compensation model, and an epigenetic model, while personally favoring a fourth historical/eschatological construct.[2] Persons charged with retiree care may gain insight from Gerkin's work. His first three models are psychological and sociocultural in nature. His *symmetrical* model is based on an image of life as "a peak between two valleys." The human life cycle is akin to a convex lens with points of the lens symbolizing life's beginning and ending phases, with "fullness of life" in adolescence and adulthood.

Relative to retirement, the center of the lens signifies one's vital, generative, expansive years of employment. Such a schema points to the inevitable decline of energy in elderhood, the anguish of pain, the limitations of the physical body, and the inevitability of death. This view of life's progression/regression, controlled by the "biological clock," is widely held in Western cultures. Persons ministering to retirees, who hold this view, practice a sustaining or supportive care style.

The late psychologist Paul Pruyser, who directed the educational enterprise at the Menninger Clinics, formerly in Topeka (relocated to Houston), proposed a *loss/compensation* model of aging. He expanded the peak/valleys construct by focusing on *being* instead of *do-*

ing issues. Rather than underscoring the deficits of growing older, Pruyser suggested six compensations of aging.[3] For retirees, the application features one's ability to redefine one's status in personal rather than instrumental terms. He encouraged retirees to live in the present moment and to practice the vital religious faith that had sustained them in the past.

Pruyser introduced a positive note into the ethos of caring for retirees, regardless of age. Rather than an overriding sense of life's diminishments and disengagements, caregivers are encouraged to nurture retirees' realistic optimism. Facilitating strengths for future tasks, relationships, and hoped-for outcomes focuses on unrealized possibilities as people live forward.

Erik Erikson's *ground plan* model of human growth through eight overlapping stages offers care providers a third option. Rather than expansion/diminishment, the late psychoanalyst pictured the human life cycle through eight stages from infancy to late adulthood.[4] He assigned a specific task to each developmental stage, with an accompanying moral virtue. The process of maturation moves ideally, Erikson held, from Infancy, with a task of forming basic trust versus mistrust, through six definable stages, into Mature Age, with a task of developing integrity versus despair. Trust and integrity for healthy retirees are conjoined and, with lifelong experience and reflection, should yield accrued wisdom for oneself and generations following.

Erikson held that failure to accomplish a stage-specific task placed an extra burden on a person. He or she would be obliged to compensate (backtrack) by seeking to accomplish a previous task, while, at the same time, tackling a new age-specific task. Harvard psychologist Robert Coles, Erikson's biographer, explained: "We do not acquire trust and forever rid ourselves of mistrust or 'achieve' autonomy and thus spare ourselves continuing doubts and hesitations."[5] Ministries with retirees, based on Erikson's epigenetic ground plan, will provide both guidance and coaching toward life's transcendence and moral obligation to model healthy living for future generations.

Gerkin proposed what he termed a *historical/eschatological* model as a fourth lens for viewing aging and pastoral care approaches with mature adults. The German theologian Jurgen Moltmann, author of *The Theology of Hope,* had served for a time as guest professor at Candler School of Theology.[6] Through his classroom lectures and conversations with faculty colleagues, Moltmann influenced Gerkin to embrace an open-ended vision of the future God is bringing about. Persons are finite, historical beings, anchored in the present scheme of things, but are free to take a long view of history—beyond time, toward eternity.

Given an eschatological perspective, retirees freely embrace dreams of their future living arrangements, companions, financial status, health maintenance, and carefree activities. Living with an eternal perspective, noted Gerkin, "*hopes* [wishes or desires] for the self's future move to the arena of participation in the great *hope* of humankind found in the Christian eschatological vision. . . . Historical self-limits thus come up against the limitlessness of God's eschatological future."[7] Such a hopeful perspective reminds us of the Apostle Paul's assurance to Christians in the ancient city of Colosse who had begun a spiritual journey by faith. "You died, and your life is now hidden with Christ in God" (Col. 3:3, NIV).

Aging and retirement, interpreted within such a historical/eschatological paradigm, is thus aging "in God," in the view of Jurgen Moltmann.[8] Gerkin's first three models of aging and pastoral care in response to aging are earth-bound psychological categories. The fourth model is theologically grounded and offers a faith perspective to retirees and liberating challenges for their religious caregivers. We shall anticipate elaborating practical applications of this *future story* model in chapters that follow. With this methodological frame of reference in mind, we turn to what retirees may anticipate when looking down the road and living forward.

LOOKING DOWN THE ROAD

A common fault in retirement planning is making stopgap decisions instead of anticipating the future with careful objectives and achievable goals in mind. Long-range planning is a requisite for both potential retirees and faith-based institutions that propose meaningful ministries with retired persons. Here, we are considering issues common to both groups, with spiritual wisdom for successful retirement and effective caring ministry.

People today are heart-hungry for a purpose to live.[9] Early in my career, I purposed *to make an impact for God on my generation*. That bold objective has served as a spiritual mandate for my entire adult life. My purpose was akin to the Apostle Paul's reference to king David, when speaking before a mixed Jewish and Gentile audience on an early missionary journey: "For when David had served God's purpose in his own generation, he fell asleep. . . ." (Acts 13:36a, NIV). Israel's most illustrious king had pointed his life to achieving God's purposes on earth.

Are you thinking about retiring? If your answer is "yes," what should you be considering? Here are selected retirement issues that require careful mapping and decision making:

- *Retirement itself.* A person anticipating life after work should think of retiring *to,* not simply from, something. In my case, it required courage to let go of job security with dependable income, plan new living arrangements, and redirect personal and social interests and priorities. Little did I know that a frightening angina health experience would occur soon after I retired.
- *Living arrangements.* Consider living in less space with less "stuff," essential living requirements, availability of medical care, distances from friends and family, and local tax laws. For various reasons, many seniors are creating unique retirement-living arrangements. Think about the following true story.

  Mary Kemp, seventy-six, and Leon Tanner, seventy-nine, are lifelong friends who planned and constructed a house to serve their special interests and unmarried partner lifestyles. They are both writers and have known each other since the early 1930s. Kemp is widowed with grown children; Tanner never married. They live in a 4,000 square foot ranch-style house with wheelchair-accessible design.[10] The roommates share a common kitchen, dining room, and living room, but they have separate living quarters, with offices, bedrooms, baths, and storage areas. Although not a duplex, it is really two houses in one. With offices nearby, they chat about writing and enjoy life as a "family."
- *Finances.* Take note of your average monthly expenses for the past two or so years; determine requirements; then budget for prospective income streams and anticipated expenses. Health care costs will predictably rise with needs for medications, possible surgeries, and various therapies. Consult an attorney about estate planning, preparing a will, signing a living will for health care, and designating a power of attorney in the event you face the inability to care for your affairs.

Advisors offering guidance about aspects of financial planning abound. Sheryl Garrett, of Shawnee Mission, Kansas, and a group of financial planners have published a question-and-answer guide for middle-income families: *Just Give Me the Answer$.*[11] Ms. Garrett and colleagues discuss questions such as, How much money will I need to retire? What is an annuity and how does it work? Should I start collecting Social Security at age sixty-two? What is a trust? The answers to these questions and others are detailed and easy to understand.

- *Health-aging-death issues.* Illness and accidents come with the aging process. Careful habits of diet, exercise, and regular physical examinations can help you stay well and detect or prevent common diseases such as breast, prostate, and colon cancer. Early warnings, such as a diagnosis of cancer or heart disease, remind us that death is personal and inevitable. You are your body; thus addressing health matters is not morbid but realistic.

- *The possibility of a second or third career.* Ronald Manheimer, executive director of the Center for Creative Retirement at the University of North Carolina in Asheville, tells the story of a friend whose image of retirement was not realistic.[12] He had dabbled in art when he was younger and wanted a second career as an artist. He discovered in his first postretirement art class that the work was much more technical and demanding than he had imagined. Although he struggled through the course, he realized art was not his gift. The emotional cost was devastating. He failed at what he imagined would be fun.

To avoid such disasters, Manheimer suggests doing some "field testing" of your retirement plans *before* you retire. Experience helps the prospective retiree *get real*. If a pilot second career fails, life does not end. That failed project can be laid aside and replaced by exploring other interests.

Charting goals to reach one's basic retirement objectives requires intelligent inquiry, prayerful dependence on God, consultation with family and trusted advisors, and common sense wisdom. You must take charge of your own life.

TAKE CHARGE OF YOUR LIFE

Retired persons move through definable life cycle phases that determine their levels of physical and mental functioning, socialization skills, self-care capabilities, technology skills, health, and faith matters. Some time frames are necessary in any approach to retirement because of cultural practices, individual differences, and the likelihood of unexpected events. Although the following time frames are flexible (and there are exceptions to this typology), they may help you to develop realistic expectations. A person may anticipate living twenty to thirty years after first retiring, with relative degrees of engagement, depending on changes in environment, companions, nutrition, health, financial resources, medical facilities, support community, and the *givens* of one's personality (such as hopefulness or pessimism).

The Young Old: From About Age Fifty-Five to Seventy-Five

At this season of life, younger retirees may still be working, volunteering, traveling, and leading active lifestyles. At some point they will experience personal health problems, have surgeries, and face the deaths of peers, friends, a spouse, or relatives. Here is a man, for example, whose early 1950s' former business associate was found unconscious on the bathroom floor. Because of all his wife and the local fire department paramedic team did to help, the man survived, but he had minimal brain function. He lives in total dependence on his spouse as a "walking dead man."

The fragility of existence dawns on retirees during this developmental phase—from the brevity of life, to disappointments with children, to concerns with their elderly parents' welfare. Given good health, couples may enjoy satisfying, although reduced, sexual activity in these years. Given their past lifestyles, the "young old" may continue to socialize; travel; participate in church, synagogue, or temple worship; and support worthy causes with time, talents, and financial assets.

The Middle Old—From About Seventy-Five to Eighty-Five

Some reduction in physical stamina, with consequent cutbacks in activity, are evident during the second phase of elderhood. Here, one's health becomes the key to true wealth. Hopefully, what assets a person foregoes will be replaced by more suitable physical and emotional activities. Cherished relatives and friends, like one's own good health, may be lost. Changes may occur in living arrangements, in one's physical stamina, and in the reduced landscape of one's future story (that is, hoped for life expectancy).

Pastoral counselor James N. Lapsley notes that "persons in this age group must make choices about continuing activity and relative disengagement on an ongoing basis."[13] A friend in his early eighties stumbled while walking and fell. He had stubbed his toe on an uneven spot in the sidewalk. "Lord, why me?!" he protested. Later, upon reflection, he did self-talk: "Stupid, if you pick up your feet, you won't fall." The lesson? Take charge of your own life. At this season of life, religious care providers, family members, and health care professionals should encourage appropriate activity but respect a person's essential limitations.

The Frail Elderly—From About Eighty-Five to Death

Retirees in this phase of the life cycle remain as active as health, desire, an available support community, and a passion for life permit. Here is a ninety-four-year-old retired historian, for example, who addresses civic club members on captivating topics. Once, the oldest working American, a man 106 years of age, was featured on a national TV network vignette. These are the exceptions to elderly retirees who must disengage from many, if not most, responsibilities. Tasks—such as paying one's bills, filing income tax statements, shopping for necessities, making and keeping medical and dental appointments, preparing meals, maintaining a household and personal cleanliness—all may require family care, nursing assistance, or institutional care.

Disabilities as varied as macular degeneration to dementia, and medical procedures from joint replacement to heart bypass surgery, take a toll on elderly retirees' energy levels and enthusiasm for life. The upper limit of aging is finite, only moderately responsive to medical therapies, such as hormone manipulation, and environmental modifications. Factors such as DNA, environment, and life-robbing diseases, such as Altzheimer's, affect human longevity. A man, reported to have achieved the fourteenth decade of life, was once interviewed by scientists in a Peruvian Andes village. At the other extreme, the AIDS epidemic in many African nations hastens the deaths of millions of middle-age adults, leaving an inverted population pyramid of children at its base and the elderly at its pinnacle.

This typology, although not universally applicable, helps caregivers distinguish the assets and deficits of people in diverse post-retirement situations. Through research, improved medical care, nutrition, aerobic exercise, and technological advances, our world culture is getting older in *chronological* age but younger in *functional* age. A combination of physical, psychological, spiritual, environmental, and social factors is reshaping society's attitude toward *social* and *functional* ages.

An important emphasis of this discussion is to focus on retiree strengths and relationships that point to favorable, positive outcomes. The stories that follow demonstrate the value of family support and connections for a retiree's emotional health and decision-making skills, the importance of community involvement in personal and public safety, and the value of belonging to a religious group that may encourage self-esteem, spiritual growth, and volunteer service. Such lifestyle assets build on strengths and ensure greater likelihood of healthy elderhood.

Some older persons no longer feel appreciated by family members. Others fear they are a nuisance to friends, physicians, and care providers. In mapping your prospective retirement landscape, ask yourself: How am I old?

HOW AM I OLD?

Mabel and Ron were both ninety-one—retired educators with different views of aging that had been shaped by images they each had carried into their later years. Their basic difference was gender, but the most essential determinants of their coming to terms with life were health and attitude. Mabel had taught mathematics and physics in a university college of engineering. Now, she enjoyed good health, stayed socially active, drove her own car, and maintained reasonable control of her life. Ron, on the other hand, was legally blind, a widower whose family had greatly benefited from his generosity. His daughter and son-in-law had placed Ron in an assisted-living center. Having signed a power of attorney over to his daughter, he felt helpless to change his surroundings or to alter his circumstances.

There are two distinct life views reflected in the way four small words are arranged in one's thinking: "How old am I?" and "How am

I old?" Psychologists tell us we each have a "child within," made up of all our experiences and memories since childhood. This inner child of the past imprints a path of basic characteristics we carry into adulthood. Some observers of the aging process feel we also have an "elder within," composed of all the stereotypes and impressions we hold about retirement and our later years. A prevailing stereotype, contributing to ageism (akin to sexism and racism), is that when you retire you are OLD.

Age Wave founder Ken Dychtwald has noted breakthroughs, such as gene therapy, supernutrition, and bionics, that may enhance one's later years. If the expectations you have of long life are filled with optimism, images of pleasant companions, rewarding activities, and feelings of usefulness, you may actually anticipate living forward.[14] To the contrary, if you envision your later years as a time of ill health—feeling useless, bored, lonely, and depressed—you may unconsciously drift in those directions.

Inevitably, aspects of life we do not control affect the outcome of retirement for good or ill. These include the country of one's birth, matters of health, social customs (for example, many Asian and African tribal groups honor the elders in their midst), family ties, political climate, financial resources, times of war or peace, and immigration and related dislocations. Persons living in the comfort zone of upper-class income tend to have healthier diets, better insurance coverage, superior medical care, more options, and greater social support than older persons in impoverished circumstances.

In his *The Virtues of Aging,* former president Jimmy Carter relates some of the experiences he and Rosalynn had following his defeat in 1980 by the late Ronald Reagan.[15] He was only fifty-six years old when he was involuntarily retired from his position of leadership in the White House. Being a "former president" in the tiny hamlet of Plains, Georgia, after years of living in the nation's capital, traveling the world, and consulting with world leaders, was not easy. His wife, Rosalynn, was especially bitter, unable to accept his loss of the 1980 election. Meanwhile, their friends noted that more than a third of American men his age were retired; furthermore, he might expect to live into his eighties. Together, they faced a most disturbing question: What would they do with the next twenty-five years?

The good fortune of having been a former "first family" in the United States favored the Carters' retirement adaptation. They were blessed with strong, supportive family members, along with a dependable staff of federal security officers. Carter noted that their mothers and other relatives, still in Plains (which had been their only real home since they were born), helped them transition back into the peanut-farming community. Their strong religious faith and a willingness to explore new commitments were factors in favor of forming more positive attitudes. Opportunities to speak, write, travel, teach, and render public service opened to them. In time, the Carter Library would open in Atlanta, and he would see service as an international peacemaker.

Jimmy and Rosalynn Carter addressed the question, "How am I old?" with a positive attitude, deeply spiritual lifestyle, creative volunteer endeavors, and a desire to live forward. In the process, they became model retirement pioneers.

Retirees face numerous myths and stereotypes about aging in America regardless of when or how they relinquish full-time employment. You have seen the list: retirees are old; most older people are in poor health; "You can't teach an old dog new tricks"; older persons are drones in a working society; older persons are uninterested in matters of sexuality; and the clincher—all older people are pretty much alike. Gene Cohen, director of the Center on Aging, Health and Humanities at George Washington University, debunks harmful myths about aging and proposes emotional foundations for hopeful living in his *The Creative Age*.[16]

How you and I answer the question, "How am I old?" will be determined largely by five factors: our health and environmental circumstances, companions and support community, attitude (optimistic or pessimistic outlook), financial considerations, and personal faith and religious worldview. Hopefully, life's chances will enable you to live with vitality, usefulness, and hopefulness to a ripe old age.

A SUMMARY OF KEY POINTS

- Retiree caregivers were provided a theoretical framework for ministry based on a typology suggested by the late Charles Gerkin, former Professor of Pastoral Theology at Candler School of Theology in Atlanta, Georgia. Rather than traditional age- or ability-related formulas of human development and decline,

Gerkin advocated a hopeful eschatological model based on a biblical worldview. I am drawn to such a *future story* perspective, reflected in the theme "living forward."

- Next, I suggested that in mapping the retirement landscape pre-retirees look realistically at retirement issues, such as retirement itself, living arrangements, availability of a dependable support community, finances, health-aging-death issues, and the possibility of a second or third career.
- In the "take charge of your life" section, I considered a process view of becoming retired. Rather than one final event, retirement was viewed as a series of choices, disengagements, and continuing activities. Three major epochs of seniority—the young old, the middle old, and the frail elderly—were pictured with potential needs and requirements for effective adaptation.
- In order to provoke reflection by potential retirees, I posed a rhetorical question, "How am I old?" Although illustrations were provided of life's limits and possibilities, each reader was encouraged to provide his or her own responses to the question. We turn, next, to the retiree's newly aroused sensitivity to the calendar and clock, with suggestions for managing time when one no longer has a structured schedule.

Chapter 4

Challenges of Managing the Calendar, Clock, and Commitments

Years ago, I recall reading the autobiographical testimony of World War II death camp survivor Viktor E. Frankl, first published with the title *From Death-Camp to Existentialism*. As a longtime prisoner in German concentration camps, all dignities of rational, humane existence were stripped from him. His father, mother, brother, and his wife died in camps or were killed in gas ovens. One wonders how this brave man—cut off from home and family, identified only with a prison number, every possession lost, suffering physical cold and psychic brutality—viewed time or found a reason to live. Yet, he survived!

Frankl not only survived the extreme suffering and deprivations with prisoners in camps such as Auschwitz and Dachau, he began to develop a system of existential analysis called *logotherapy*. Once, during an American lecture tour, I heard the Austrian psychotherapist describe how men, trapped in the meaninglessness of timeless existence, survived because of a rich inner life, profound religious faith, vivid memories of the past, and hope-filled images of the future.

Separated from his family, Frankl did not know his wife had died. It was his love for her and vivid images of her that "set a seal upon his heart"—love stronger than death. "Love goes . . . beyond the physical person of the beloved," wrote Frankl. "It finds its deepest meaning in his [her] spiritual being, his [her] inner self."[1] His strength to love nurtured his will to live and helped him to survive.

During one evening's lecture, Frankl described how his "will to meaning" helped him endure while working one gray dawn in a Bavarian prison camp. He was trying to recall images of his beloved wife while searching for a reason for his sufferings—his slow dying.

Spiritual Wisdom for Successful Retirement
Published by The Haworth Press, Inc. 2006. All rights reserved.
doi:10.1300/5537_05

Looking up momentarily through the semidarkness, as though by divine intervention, he saw a light in a distant farmhouse. It appeared painted on the horizon. A light was shining in the darkness! It became a defining moment; it sparked within a renewed reason to live.

From such experiences—from choosing to see beauty beyond ugliness, from hoping that, somehow, he would have a future, and drawing upon spiritual resources—Frankl sought to make sense of suffering. When the prisoners were finally liberated, he walked from the camp toward a nearby town. Later, he wrote of falling to his knees and praying the one sentence he always kept in mind: "I called to the Lord from my narrow prison and He answered me in the freedom of space."[2]

In time, Frankl developed an existential theory, which he named *Logos* therapy (logotherapy), to help persons beyond the morass of meaningless existence. *Logos,* the Greek word that denotes "meaning," transcends logic, held Frankl. He believed that a person's search for meaning in an existential vacuum is a fact, not merely wishful thinking. His experience taught him that humankind's core values and ideals may inspire a search for meaning and *pull*, not push, such persons toward the future.

Why examine a death-camp prisoner's experience in a discussion of calendar and clock, you may wonder? Like the concentration camp captives, we are immersed in time like fish are in water. The emotionally healthy person knows there is no escape from life. Like hope and love, time and life are four-letter words, picturing intangibles that interpenetrate each other. Retirees face closures and beginnings—netted in the mesh of time. Leaving paid employment does not free a retiree from occasional feelings of bring trapped or relieve a person from tasks of managing the endless demands of time, amid interruptions, in a hurry-up world.

HAVE YOU SLOWED DOWN YET?

It is a perfectly legitimate question. An out-of-state friend, a couple of years younger than am I, asked me that question a few months into my retirement journey. "Have you slowed down yet?" With a reputation as a workaholic, driven like many of my fellow Americans with the Puritan work ethic, his probe brought me up short. It was not a rebuke, only a friendly reminder that retired persons in life's seventh decade have earned the right to rest.

Coming to terms with one's *temporality* in retirement re-stirs the time-consciousness one may have experienced in earlier stages of development. Rather than the open road of youth, a retiree's time landscape narrows with an inevitable end in view. Now, life must be evaluated by different criteria than achieving success in one's vocation, facing poverty, creating wealth, performing civic duties, owning the right vehicle, or winning a prized contest. Adolescent questions about identity and meaning may beg for reconsideration in later years. Like Lewis Carroll's Alice, struggling with the identity question, retirees ask: "But if I'm not the same, the next question is, 'who in the world am I?'"[3] Wise retirees often reflect on all that has gone before while trying to stay connected and break the unknown future code.

Aging demands answers for new concerns because nostalgia is not a strategy for hope-filled, futuristic living. New tasks may beckon: enriching one's inner life with reading, travel, renewed appreciation of nature and the arts; focusing on a second career; engaging socially with one's peers; learning to play a sport such as golf; or developing a deepened spiritual sensitivity. Health maintenance may become a major concern, with time-consuming trips to a hospital or rehabilitation center. A retiree is connected to all that he or she has been, met, and experienced in the past yet anticipates all that God has in store for a fulfilling, useful future.

The Creator of us all invites contemplation—"Be still and know that I am God; I will be exalted among the nations, I will be exalted in the earth" (Ps. 46:10, NIV). It takes a firm act of will to affirm with the ancient psalmist: "My times are in [God's] hands" (Ps. 31:15, NIV). The Hebrew word for *be still* carries the force of "stop, enough!" Our Maker invites us to passionate discovery of new dimensions of the triune God. We should not wait until we or someone dear to us has a critical illness, major surgery, heart attack, or crippling accident to ask if we are living as God intends. *Slowing down* becomes the work of giving up old grudges, bestowing forgiveness, enjoying beauty, enriching relationships, and envisioning the future.

Rather than facing Viktor Frankl's closed-time system in a German concentration camp, most retirees are free to choose how they will spend their days.

A DAY IN THE LIFE OF A RETIREE

Typically, there is seldom a *typical* day for a retired person, because each individual is unique and circumstances and contexts differ. Some should-be retired persons still go to work each day. A mid-nineties attorney friend is at his office desk by 6:30 a.m. each morning. Evelyn Johnson, a ninety-five-year-old flight instructor still teaches every day. When asked how long she planned on working, she said as long as she still had the passion, she would continue to fly.[4] A seventy-seven-year-old Mississippi native was lauded for staying the course twenty years, instructing at Tarrant County Community College and showing no signs of stopping. She teaches drama and vocabulary, coordinates museum tours, recruits faculty, and guides the senior education program on the TCCC Northwest Campus.[5]

Other persons are slowed from a typical day's activities by some debilitating illness, accident, or malady. A woman who normally spent much of each day caring for her Alzheimer's-afflicted husband ended as a hospital patient herself. She had forgotten that she had placed a small table by her ailing husband's chair, turned suddenly to retrace her steps, fell over the table, and broke her hip. A cancer survivor, the woman's faith in God, iron will, and support from church friends and neighbors kept things at home relatively normal until she recuperated.

Seventy-nine-year-old William Manchester, author of a popular biography of Sir Winston Churchill, was felled by two strokes. The first two volumes of an intended trilogy, *Visions of Glory* (1983) and *Alone* (1988), were best sellers. The final manuscript, *The Last Lion,* of which Manchester completed 237 pages, lies unfinished. "Language for me came as easily as breathing for fifty years, (but) I can't do it anymore," confessed Manchester during an interview at his Middletown, New York, home. "The feeling is indescribable." Time's course has retired the noted literary genius. His enfeeblement serves as a metaphor for life's brevity.

Retirees of sound mind and good physical health are typically intentional in planning a day, a month, or a future experience. Events unfold among interruptions, unexpected phone calls, and the day's simplified tasks, such as preparing meals, eating (often alone), reading the daily newspaper, viewing television news reports or favorite programs, running errands, entertaining guests, and (often a highlight) reading the day's mail. If one is still able to drive safely and is legally licensed to drive, the retiree may drive to shop, keep a medical or dental appointment, or visit a hair salon. For mobility-impaired persons, a public conveyance is required.

Infants are born into the world without a watch. Although they are conscious of light and sound, they have no awareness of time per se. Hunger pains? Yes. Discomforts? Yes. An infant, however, never checks a clock or calendar. We have to be taught to *tell time* and to learn the stern lessons of human temporality. It is reported that King Philip of Macedonia, father of Alexander the Great, assigned a servant to announce to him each dawn: "Remember that you must die."

The logistics of retirement are illogical. No matter how carefully scheduled a person's day—arising at about the same time, perhaps enjoying private worship (through devotional reading, meditation, or prayerful reflection), breakfasting, toileting, dressing (this may become multiple tasks according to the person's scheduled obligations), walking or exercising, attending to one's pet or potted plants, and so on—interruptions occur. A trip to the post office often involves waiting in line to be served. Driving in city traffic involves waiting for traffic signals to change, for a siren-sounding ambulance or fire engine to pass, or while an accident ahead is cleared from the intersection. Social engagements and entertainment events nip at one's bank of time. Correspondence, whether by hand or computer, requires attention. One has to pay bills, keep records, file documents, and, in season, compute taxes (often with assistance) for the IRS.

A day in the life of disadvantaged or ill retirees, doing life from the underside, may be quite restricted. Activities may be determined by health needs: cardiac, speech, or inhalation rehabilitation therapy; kidney dialysis; waiting for a volunteer to deliver a meal on wheels; or receiving visits from a home health nurse. Here is a Hispanic grandmother, standing in line at a Catholic Charities Center, awaiting food distribution for her unemployed husband and herself. A couple may have traveled hundreds of miles to arrive at a diagnostic center, then wait hours for an appointment with a respected physician or for an essential technical examination.

Instead of being free to "do as they please," many retired persons feel a new kind of *time bind*—confined in the clutches of calendar and clock. They simply mark time, awaiting some hoped-for visitor and watching the days and seasons slip by.

HOW TO AVOID A FRITTERED EXISTENCE

Some theologians hold that pride (ego) leads to the average person's downfall. I beg to differ and propose that one of the greatest temptations for retirees is yielding to a frittered existence. Time just "gets away" and disappears. Intending to achieve some long-cherished goal—such as mastering the computer, learning a second language, visiting an old friend, traveling overseas, or chronicling a self-history—many retirees experience a haphazard lifestyle. Pursuing small talk with neighbors and friends, volunteering for some worthwhile cause, caring for an ailing relative, paying bills, caring for a tiny garden spot, visiting dentists and physicians, reading a book, or working crossword puzzles—time just gets away.

Anthropologist Margaret Mead once noted that what people say, what people do, and what they say they do are entirely different things. Have you ever wondered how to set boundaries for your precious days or how to accept a discipline? The place to begin a focused life is with yourself. You are your own best friend or worst enemy when it comes to setting priorities and accomplishing objectives. Questions concerning the meaning of life override the "how-tos" of time usage. Here are some guidelines to help you use your time, energy, and resources to the best advantage.

- *Set achievable goals in line with your priorities.* The time line of life appears shorter the older we get. Still, it makes sense to have long-term, intermediate, and short-term goals. Are you a list maker? Jot it down. Do you use a computer or a PDA-type device? A tiny, hand-held transmitter can serve as a telephone, calendar/date book, Internet outlet, and camera. Just enter your data. We must aim at a goal in order to reach the target.
- *Do it today.* Delays can become deadening. Procrastination ("I'll get around to that tomorrow") leaves the retiree with a dangling promise. Resolve to handle paperwork once, not over and over. Someone has said, "The road to hell is paved with good intentions." Wanting to begin an exercise program, planning to lose weight, getting that annual physical examination (but postponing it), thinking about a visit to Aunt May's in Vermont does not cut it. Establish wholesome routines, and aim toward your goals. Self-discipline should be a lifestyle.

- *Check your rationalizations.* We are all skilled at making excuses. Nature protects us with sophisticated, unconscious defense mechanisms. It is one thing to take a disciplined and devoted delay concerning some matter, such as moving from a large residence and lawn requiring upkeep into a condominium or assisted-living center. It is another thing to excuse yourself and then, in time, to be forced by a crisis to act with restricted options. Make certain the excuse you rationalize for delaying a key decision or making a choice is valid.
- *Our decisions become deeds.* For my entire professional life I have recorded each day's major events, accomplished tasks, correspondence, and key phone calls in a date book. Now, as memory slips, I know where yesterday or last week went. "But doesn't note-making require time?" you wonder. Yes, a bit, but there is the rewarding pleasure of knowing what has occurred or is scheduled ahead. Our plans, decisions, and actions become deeds we can see.

Some readers may desire to move beyond broad guidelines to specifics. How, in the real world, may a retired person move from a frittered existence to a workable plan? At least some of the following suggestions may prove useful for you:

1. Learn to handle projects once. Note any unfinished goals from previous days and list them under URGENT or OTHER priorities for the next day or week.
2. Consolidate scattered messages so you are free to discard paper scraps, notes on the backs of used envelopes, old grocery lists, and reminders of intended tasks.
3. Become aware of the length of time you are spending during telephone conversations, on the computer, watching television, playing bingo or cards so that you are keeping, not merely killing, time.
4. Distinguish rumination and worrying from praying and planning. To ruminate is primarily to replay old or faulty mental "tapes" when things have gone amiss.
5. Make certain you are attempting reasonable tasks, given your age and health. Delegate tasks that are too risky or difficult, or employ helpers when tasks have become too demanding or

health threatening. One frail elderly woman's niece came to her house each week to aid with chores that had become too difficult for her.

6. Practice patience and provide for infinite flexibility. Service personnel who make house calls frequently fail to keep previously scheduled appointments. If the appointment is "stale," call the individual or his employer a day or two in advance to remind him or her that an appearance is scheduled. Remember, interruptions happen. Cut people "some slack." Like you, they are more human than otherwise.

There are meaning-filled issues that probe deeper than calendaring ideas.

HOW DO YOU SPEND YOUR SABBATH?

The ancient Jewish *sabbath* was modeled on God's rest following the six days of creation. The Hebrew text notes that, after "the heavens and the earth were completed in all their vast array," God rested on the seventh day of creation. Eugene H. Peterson reminds us that the Hebrew understanding of day and week is not our perception. "And there was evening and there was morning, one day . . ." on and on, repeated six times in the Genesis account. *Day,* Peterson noted in *Working the Angles,* is the basic unit of God's creative work, and evening is the beginning of that day.[6] Notice, "God blessed the seventh day and made it holy, because on it he rested from all the work of creating that he had done" (Gen. 2:1-3, NIV).

The Sabbath's significance was underscored at Mount Sinai, when God handed Moses Ten Commandments as enduring guidelines for obedient living. The first four commands are vertically related to humankind's God-relationship; the last six instructions involve duties to one's parents and neighbors. The bridge commandment reads: "Remember the Sabbath day by keeping it holy. Six days you shall labor and do all your work, but the seventh day is a Sabbath to the Lord your God" (Exod. 20:8, NIV). Sabbath observance embodies an ontological obligation.

In Deuteronomy 5:12-15 one finds another reason for Sabbath observance. During 400 years of slavery in Egypt, the Israelites' ancestors had no time free from labor. The enslaved Jews were overworked and dehumanized. Thus, the Sabbath day was to be received as God's gift for rest, worship, and reflection. We are to stop work, quit what we have been doing for six working days, and take a break. "Remembering the day" ensures rehumanizing experiences.

The Sabbath, ideally, affords time—however it is achieved—to practice the presence of God. The guideline applies to all humankind. "It means entering realms of spirit where wonder and adoration have space to develop, where play and delight have time to flourish."[7] In our hurry-up, quick delivery, sound-bite culture, the notion of taking time out for worship, reflection, rest, and relaxation seems antiquated. Some people imagine it works for monks and nuns in monasteries, for hermits in desert places, and for persons "of the cloth" who are far removed from life's realities.

The question is eternally relevant: "How do you spend your Sabbath?" We are to keep the Sabbath holy in order to remember, honor, and thank God, to replenish the human spirit, to enjoy occasions of solitude and re-create through worship. History cautions us, continue to break the Sabbath and the violated Sabbath breaks you. The New Testament says of Jesus the Christ that he periodically "drew aside" for prayer, rest, and fellowship with his friends. Because the incarnate God kept the Sabbath, in the days of his flesh, can we do less?

Sabbath-keeping in all its contemporary expressions is more than a matter of choice—of "what to do" with one's *day off.* It is a theological obligation with eternal consequences. Remembering the Creator—taking Sabbath time for God—orbits the six other days around the Eternal. No wonder the Bible admonishes: "Put your hope in God," not in some magical force called *luck,* for hope is the supreme antidote to anomie and despair (e.g., NIV, Job 13:15; Ps. 42:5, 147:11; Isa. 40:31; Rom. 5:4; Heb. 11:1).

LIVING IN HOPE

We began this discussion with the inspirational example of Viktor Frankl's spiritual transformation from World War II death-camp deprivations, brutalities, and deaths into existential realism. His rich inner life, religious faith, vivid memories of his wife (whom he did not know was dead), and hope-filled images of the future enabled him to survive the horrors of German death camps. You may ask wistfully, but what of the thousands of prisoners who died miserably despite all the hopes they held dear? A true believer could argue that the prisoners who died were sustained by hope and prayer in their martyrdom. There is no such thing as "idle hope." Their hopefulness, although they were tortured and finally defeated, inspired other prisoners (such as Viktor Frankl) who were ultimately freed.

Annie Dillard was right: how we spend our days is how we spend our lives. This book's theme of *living forward* can become your reality as you live each day hoping in God. Hopefulness is a personal choice and a social force. Living in hope correlates with a plan of action that a person or community holds. Hope is neither wishful thinking nor mere optimism, because optimism may be unwilling to face reality. Hope, along with other great realities, such as faith, love, work, and play, noted the late psychiatrist Karl Menninger, lies at the center of emotional health.[8] Indeed, the Hebrew-Christian scriptures note that "we are saved by hope" (Rom. 8:24, NIV).

Retirees and those care providers who sojourn alongside them are called to hope in the thickness of life, which, at times, is like living in a river of molasses. To be a minister, rabbi, health care provider, family member, neighbor, or friend—seeking to attend or support a troubled retiree—may feel, at times, like kayaking in white water. The hopefulness envisioned here is not merely feeling lucky or the Pollyannaism of looking at life's events through rose-colored glasses. Hopefulness is not the same thing as cheerfulness, or denial of reality, or pretending to be happy. Rather, I am advocating biblical hope in God—confidence in God's future already ahead of us—that is truly "an anchor for the soul" (Heb. 6:19, NIV).

The human need for hope will not go away. "But how does hope work in our daily lives?" the retired person may wonder. Consider some of hope's dynamic activities, viewed metaphorically, when contrasted with the anomie of despair.

- Hope offers us the dawn of a new day despite the night's darkness.
- Hope opens new horizons and lifts the soul's skyline to a larger vision of reality.
- Hope tackles today's tasks, however simple or complex, which require attention.

- Hope endures disappointment and suffering in light of our true home with God.
- Hope stays the course, exercises faith in tough times, and finds the strength to love God and others with undiscourageable good will. Hope is stronger than death.
- Hope, to paraphrase poet Percy Shelley's *Ode to the West Wind,* scatters, like sparks from an unextinguished hearth, our words and deeds to humankind.

Biblical hope is anchored in and nurtured by Jesus Christ's incarnation, crucifixion, resurrection, and promised return. God-in-Christ, through the power of the Holy Spirit, will, someday, dwell among his elect in a new "promised land" (Rev. 21:3, NIV). Theologian Jurgen Moltmann has said it well in his *In the End—the Beginning: The Life of Hope*: "Christian hope is based once and for all on the remembrance of Christ."[9] Hope in God reaches into all our days and darkest nights, and into all our ways, not with "what if?" but, "because" divine light shines in our darkness, we do not give up.

This fact was summed up in the testimony of a dear friend who was dying. As a child, Henry had contracted rheumatic fever and a major heart valve was damaged. Slowed by his health experience, yet persisting in educational and professional achievements, he lived long enough to teach homiletics to hundreds of seminarians. Despite heart valve replacement surgery by a world-class surgeon in Houston's Texas Medical Center, he "fell upon sleep" at last. Before he died, Henry quoted a faith statement from the Apostle Paul to me: "Whether we live or die, we belong to the Lord" (Rom. 14:8, NIV).

To summarize, the human condition rests ultimately in transcendent hands—the promise of God's abiding presence in circumstances of evil, suffering, injustice, uncertainty, and death (Rom. 8:37-39, NIV).[10] Biblical faith in divine providence is the ground of human longing and realistic hoping. The Old Testament speaks more of obedience than of hope; but in the New Testament hope prevails. . . . A church, synagogue, or temple as a community of faith, ideally, is to cradle the vision and nurture the hopes of its members. The practice of pastoral care and wise counsel encourages endurance despite suffering and imperfection and seeks to inspire hopefulness through trust in God's eternal care.

A SUMMARY OF KEY POINTS

- Viktor Frankl's World War II death-camp experiences remind retirees that they, too, face endings, beginnings, and constrictions—netted in the mesh of time. His *will to meaning* and call for hope among prisoners confined within concentration camp walls inspires us all. Frankl was not satisfied simply to "do time" in a German concentration camp.

- "Have you slowed down yet?" is a perfectly legitimate question. The retiree's time landscape has narrowed with an inevitable end in view. Because nostalgia is not a strategy, what approaches are you using to ensure hope-filled living? List some new interests or tasks that beckon now that you have time off from paid employment. Inside each of us is a "child" who longs to play. You have earned the right to rest.

- If you had to describe events in a typical day of your current life, what would you include? Would you really rather be working, at least part-time at some paying job, than being an exemployee? Why? Under what circumstances did you first become aware of the urgency of the clock, calendar, and commitments?

- Questions concerning the meaning of life override the "how-to" of time usage. We each need a reason to live. What uses of your days do you practice now? From ancient times, the Sabbath day was received as God's gift to stop working, rest, worship, and reflect on things that matter. Why is it insufficient to think of the Sabbath as simply a "day off" from work? How do you spend your Sabbath?

- I suggested that living in hope correlates with a plan of action that a person or community holds. What did the biblical writer mean when he wrote "we are saved by hope" (Rom. 8:24, NIV)? It was noted that, while Viktor Frankl was sustained by hope in a German death-camp, thousands of his fellow prisoners who also hoped and prayed for release died in the prison ovens. What factors do you think shaped Frankl's hope and helped him live? Biblical faith in divine providence is the ground of human longing and realistic hoping.

- If you knew you had only six months to live, how would you spend each day?

Chapter 5

How to Deal with the Blues and the Blahs

Glenn Bryant was an unsung American hero who died with Alzheimer's disease. A man of many talents, he was, first, an effective interpreter and creative communicator of the Hebrew-Christian scriptures. He was also an advocate for disadvantaged youth, an avid outdoor sportsman, an artist, an inspiring community leader, and a trusted friend. Glenn's weekly broadcast, *Life at Its Best,* on station KALB in Alexandria, Louisiana, featured lively themes with compelling interest, humor, and inspiration.

Many listeners to his encouraging messages were homebound, unable to join worshippers in some faith community. Glenn reached people whose enthusiasm for life may have dried up. They were seekers after security, not risky adventurers. *Life at Its Best* reminded older listeners of a time when their bodies were strong and flexible, their spirits were responsive and passionate, and they were fully engaged in the marathon of life.

Listeners faced a variety of adversities—failed financial ventures, broken family ties, debilitating diseases, unfulfilled expectations, loneliness, personal betrayals, and spiritual malaise. Profound cultural and technological changes had left many of them feeling insignificant and "out of it." They had lived into a time when crime rates skyrocketed and terrorist threats turned a free society into an armed camp. They had seen family styles change, divorce become common, and interracial marriage increase tenfold since 1960. Uncontrolled immigration and cultural migration had changed America's character and religious expressions forever.

Spiritual Wisdom for Successful Retirement
Published by The Haworth Press, Inc. 2006. All rights reserved.
doi:10.1300/5537_06

Little wonder that concerned listeners were drawn to encouraging messages advocating "life at its best." The only thing wrong with the notion of "life at its best" is that, at times, really bad things happen to nice people.

DEPRESSING EVENTS HAPPEN TO THE NICEST PEOPLE

We are told that every year at least 98,000 Americans die and millions are injured as a result of medical mistakes. Consider the following incident.

> Four years ago, 15-year-old Lewis Blackman went to a hospital in Charleston, S.C., for standard surgery to correct a chest malformation—a birth defect. The operation went well, the surgeon said. But soon things began to go wrong.
>
> According to Lewis' mother, Helen Haskell, 53, a resident doctor prescribed an adult dosage of Toradol for postsurgical pain, and over the next four days Lewis received 17 doses, despite the drugmaker's recommendation not to give it to patients under 16.
>
> The boy grew weaker, unable to keep food and liquids down. Three days after the operation he suddenly developed excruciating abdominal pain. His mother says the family asked for an attending physician to examine him, but all they saw was a parade of interns and residents and nurses who prodded him to get up and walk to ease his pain.
>
> Finally, a fourth-year resident ordered a blood test. The results—delayed because the computers were down—shed little light on the case. Haskell says a blood count that would have shown bleeding or infection was never done. Lewis's condition worsened dramatically—still no physician came to see him. The boy finally died, and a day later an autopsy showed that a large duodenal ulcer had eaten a hole in his intestines. Lewis Blackman had bled to death.
>
> Nobody expects to die from medical treatment. But they do every day—and in alarming numbers. The Institute of Medicine in Washington estimates that at least 98,000 people die in hospitals each year from medical errors. And about 2 million patients

acquire infections, according to the U.S. Centers for Disease Control and Prevention. . . .[1]

Why do so many die from botched and inadequate treatment in a country that claims to have the best medical system in the world? The answer circles back to an increasingly complex system of care that was designed with efficacy, not necessarily patient safety, in mind. Ironically, as medical technology offers treatments and cures undreamed of four decades ago, safety has suffered. "Forty years ago medicine was safer but not as effective," says Robert Wachtrer, M.D., chief of medical service at the University of California San Francisco Medical Center. "These changes [in technology] require more specialized doctors, communication and teams working together." That doesn't always happen.[2]

What is Helen Haskell, Lewis Blackman's mother, doing to improve patient care in South Carolina? She is seeking legislation that would require hospitals to display the ranks of medical personnel on name badges and to give families an emergency number to call if they believe their patient is not getting proper medical attention. So far, the South Carolina Hospital Association has stymied the proposal, calling it burdensome to hospitals.[3]

Why relate narratives like those of a minister addressing "life at its best" or of a grieving mother facing life at its worst? Because both parties focused on action to address problematic issues, on the value of staying connected with family members and persons in a position to help, and on the importance of courage and faith. Their positive examples may inspire us as we consider the possibility of depression.

EVERYONE FACES ADVERSITY

Few persons face hurtful workplaces, accidents, health loss, rejection, guilt, disappointment, betrayal, or a loved one's death only once. People face *life,* all kinds of experiences, every day. Sadly, many Americans become depressed as they try to come to grips with life's rapid changes and numerous losses. Much depression is unrecognized, because it wears disguises such as addictions to alcohol, drugs, and pornography; spousal abuse; compulsive gambling; under-achievement at school; and chronic fatigue at home or work. Depression has spread most rapidly among the nation's youth, due, in part, to identification with faulty heroes, mixed-message music, chaotic social values, unsupervised Internet communication, cultural disorientation, chemical addictions, and vocational confusion.

There are multiple causes of the malady diagnosed as depression: social, psychological, biological, and spiritual. Social disturbances include factors such as the loss of neighborhoods, prevalence of urban gangs, increased violence, corporate crime by CEOs at the top of their game, and global migration with consequent linguistic, religious, and ethnic tribalism. In an effort to stem the tide of depressive reactions, drug companies have moved advertising from medical journals to consumers via television and other popular media. As a clue to emotional unrest, with associated feelings of the blues and blahs, the United States consumes 95 percent of the world's Prozac and 90 percent of the world's Ritalin.

Some researchers advocate biological causes of depression—"it's in our genes and body chemistry." We are products of our family histories, of maladies such as diabetes and attention deficit disorder, with dispositions toward addictive chemical dependence. There are psychological and spiritual aspects of the blues such as feelings of hopelessness, plaguing doubts, and feelings of shame and inappropriate guilt. When old certainties have been swept away people feel anxious and confused. Unforgiveness, unresolved anger, feeling rejected and worthless, difficulty concentrating, or suicidal thoughts may be evidences of depression.

We need to recognize that depression is not a new malady. Caring ministers recall that Job, in the oldest book of the Bible, struggled against symptoms of despair. He reasoned with his Maker: "I have been allotted months of futility, and nights of misery have been assigned to me. When I lie down I think, 'How long before I get up?' The night drags on, and I toss till dawn. . . . My days . . . come to an end without hope" (Job 7:3-4, 6, NIV). Job's resentment over his losses, sleeplessness, pained physical condition, feelings of self-pity, and mood of hopelessness are symptoms of depression.

We all have our ups and downs—our good/better and bad/worst days. Consider a real-life situation. An elderly friend stopped by the restaurant table where my wife and I were enjoying a leisurely lunch.

"How are you?" we inquired, because it had been quite a while since we had seen Betty.

"Well," she paused (as if to collect her thoughts), "I had my left breast removed two weeks ago because of a malignancy." She pointed to her left side, still healing from the surgery. "Then," she continued as if still stunned, "yesterday, Bill was involved in a serious automobile accident."

"What happened?" we asked. She explained that her mid-eighties husband was turning into a service station to buy fuel. A woman whom he failed to see came speeding down the hill and crashed into him just as he turned into the entrance. "Our car was demolished. Bill had to be rushed to the hospital emergency room. He was badly bruised and shaken, but the doctor's examination showed no broken bones. He was very fortunate."

Betty's poise while relating the incident may have been due, in part, to her professional background as a registered nurse. She had long ago learned to steel herself against critical events such as an automobile crash with problematic outcomes. Beyond professionalism, a character trait of spiritual steadfastness ran deep in her soul. Rather than collapsing in despair, she was philosophical but not whimsical. Her serenity under stress reminded me of a comment by Aeiko Hara, our Japanese tour guide, during a visit to Kyoto, Japan: "Even cherry trees have stormy nights."

Nice people experience troubles, face losses, and deal with disappointments. A downcast person both feels and looks discouraged. When an individual has "the blues" for an extended period of time, we conclude he or she may be depressed. In fact, a cluster of symptoms, beyond sadness, may become apparent to family members and friends when a person appears downhearted.

Wounded spirits "read" comments and situations incorrectly and make attributive errors. A despondent person may regard some event as resulting from an imagined cause. For example, "She attributes his bad temper to poor health." Anxious people tend to overreact to events and skew reality. They may appear angry or impatient. Questioning self-worth, they are self-depreciating and focus on failures. Dejected persons noticeably retreat from social engagements and fear criticism and rejection. Such persons may seek advice, but ignore it, and may not know they are depressed.

A DISEASE OR A DISORDER?

We find ourselves asking, is depression a medical disease, like diabetes or cancer? Is it a social problem or primarily an affective disorder? According to Anthony D'Agostino, MD, psychiatrists are uncertain whether

> depression is a disease, a scapegoat phenomenon, a problem in living, a conditioned response to a series of more or less accidental environmental contingencies, an . . . existential awareness of the futility of man's struggle against the inevitability of death, or all of the above.[4]

We are told that some depressive states simply disappear with the passing of time. This is particularly true of reactive depressions—periods of adaptation to a specific loss, grief, disablement, conflicted relationship, or post-traumatic stress syndrome caused by war, sexual assault, or injurious accident.

Just how common is this disability? Nearly 20 million Americans suffer symptoms of major depression every year. It is the fourth leading cause of death after heart disease, cancer, and traffic accidents. Twice as many women are diagnosed with the disorder as men. It is a social force, not simply a personal difficulty. The good news is that most persons disabled with depression can improve with appropriate treatment. Popping antidepressant pills such as Prozac, Paxil, and Zoloft is only part of the solution. A combination of cognitive therapy, along with carefully prescribed dosages of medication, has proved most effective.

Because patients turn first to primary care physicians, many of whom serve in managed care settings, they frequently receive prescriptions without wise counsel. Medications often treat symptoms, not causes; thus, temporary symptom relief from antidepressants alone is just that—temporary. Cognitive therapy is designed to guide sufferers in identifying, evaluating, and changing distorted thinking.

Helen Mayberg, MD, professor of psychiatry at Emory University, and colleagues at the University of Toronto recently published a study of why people may benefit more from a combination of antidepressants and therapy than from either alone. The researchers compared brain scans from people with depression who completed psychotherapy with scans from patients who were treated with Paxil alone. They discovered that the treatments do not act on the same places in the brain. According to Dr. Mayberg, "Patients who had psychotherapy had brain changes in the cortex, the brain's 'thinking structure,' while the Paxil appeared to uniquely target structures deep in the brain like the limbic system, the brain's emotion center."[5] Cognitive therapy coaches patients who are sad or angry to examine the thoughts behind their emotions, then reevaluate their life situation.

WE ARE OUR STORIES

Naturally, we wonder how ordinary people face life's complexities and come to terms with the sometimes tragic circumstances enveloping their lives. The following stories may show readers how to deal with discouragement and instruct those who sojourn alongside hurting persons how to face the blues and the blahs.

The Power of Faith Affirmed

Alma and Charles were in their sixties when Charles developed symptoms of Alzheimer's disease. Parents of two daughters, one of whom was a registered nurse, they could not depend on family care because the girls were married with families and lived far away. Alma arranged her schedule to care for Charles until he was institutionalized shortly before his death. She lived alone in their urban house, was active in her church, including singing in the senior adult choir, and served as a hospital volunteer.

Alma had many friends, was fiercely independent, physically strong, and determined to live well. The passing of time found her in her early nineties and still driving the family automobile. In time, she began to lose visual acuity and become unstable because of dizziness. Friends had to drive her for medical appointments and to purchase groceries. She failed to tell her daughters, now grandparents themselves, that she had fallen several times. In terms of human development theory, Alma had become a frail elderly member of her congregation. Eventually, she entered an assisted-living facility and died at the age of ninety-two.

It was a cold winter day when she was buried in the family cemetery plot. Family and friends alike commented on her victorious Christian faith, on how she determinedly leaned into life, and moved forward with courage. Her minister noted how, although living alone, she shrugged off advancing symptoms of aging, continued "doing" for others, manifested a sweet spirit, and modeled courage to the end.

Facing Major Illness

James and Kathy, in their late sixties, had built their dream house in an upscale gated community. Jim had been a skilled pilot in the U.S. Air Force; later, he became a minister and an encourager of young ministers. They were the parents of several children and enjoyed an extended family of grandchildren and relatives. Kathy had experienced a number of health difficulties that eventually required multiple heart bypass surgery. Her core values were profoundly spiritual, and her outlook remained positive. A talented musician, she had a ready smile, a sunny disposition, and reflected a life of healing love.

As James neared seventy, a routine physical examination revealed a tumor growing in his intestinal area. Surgically removed at a fine medical center, the self-contained tumor was malignant. Neither chemotherapy nor radiation was recommended. James recovered on schedule with his physician's instructions to lose weight and exercise regularly. He continued a heavy travel, speaking, and work schedule.

How did James avoid discouragement, you wonder? He was a visionary person, educated first as an engineer. Thus, James relished the many technological advances that modernity provided. His retirement office at home was well-supplied with computer technology and laden with replicas of planes he had flown. James' profound faith and disciplined prayer life reflected a positive relationship with his heavenly Father. That he had a delightful sense of humor, enjoyed music, had enjoyed successful careers, and traveled internationally—all enhanced his well-being and ensured his sustainability into old age.

Living Alone

It has not been easy for Billie to adapt to the loneliness she experienced following her husband's death. An independent woman in her early eighties, she had married Andy when they were in their mid-twenties. Their long and fruitful marriage was blessed not only by three highly educated, accomplished children, but by a supportive social network of colleagues and friends. Andy had been an avowed optimist, gifted with a brilliant mind, and endowed with the capacity to affirm and inspire his associates.

"I still miss him," she would say each time a close friend mentioned Andy's name. "I miss him as much today as when he died." Indeed, their lives had been intertwined through physical closeness, parenting tasks, continuing education and world travels, professional societies, and Andy's recognized achievements. Still residing in their big house, each room had symbolic reminders of her lost companion. The absence of his physical presence aggravated her feelings of loneliness. His silenced voice produced a different kind of quiet than a voice that had never been heard.[6]

Andy's spouse especially missed him when evening came. No one came home from work to share the "other" events of the day. There was no companion for table talk at meal time. Andy was not there to hear her reports of interesting telephone visits, to listen to her read excerpts from a letter in the day's mail, or to share a television program together. Billie ached in her soul because she had lost her best friend, and, at her stage in life, there was no companion to take his place.

"What saved Billie from disconsolation and eventual depression?" you wonder. Fortunately, she was a woman of faith, highly literate, with a network of neighbors, friends, and supportive children. A woman of substance, she maintained civic memberships gained during Andy's lifetime, attended Bible study and worship services regularly as an active church member, and sought to keep his memory alive as best she could. Through hosting friends, visiting her children and grandchildren in other parts of the country, and consulting regularly with several medical specialists, Billie lived a balanced, engaged life.

We might ask, "What have we learned by considering these real-life stories?" We realize that experiencing Alzheimer's disease, heart bypass surgery, cancer, or losing one's companion and living alone may put a person and his or her family at risk for depression. Any imbalance in a key area of life, whereby you are unable to find emotional and spiritual resources to cope with the demands of the events, may become the harbinger of depression. Your positive attitudes and adaptive skills to life's experiences serve as internal resources that build on hope and defy discouragement.

Their positive models of adaptation to life events avoided some of the chief indicators of depression:

- Feelings of hopelessness or loneliness—"no one cares"—"there's no future."
- Obvious changes in sleeping or eating patterns, social relations, or sexual desires.
- Waking tired or experiencing chronic fatigue—feeling "I just can't go on like this."
- Waves of sadness—feeling trapped, with no way out of a dilemma or conflict.

When such symptoms seem extreme or endure for an unreasonable time, a person and his or her companions need to seek appropriate assistance.

STAYING WELL IS AN INSIDE JOB

How, then, can you deal with the blues and blahs? You may have heard of Dr. Meyer Friedman, author of *Type "A" Behavior and Your Heart*. A cardiologist, Friedman observed that his heart patients' behavior was characterized by perfectionism, time urgency, competitiveness, impatience, and drivenness. He noted that high-achieving, idealistic persons who experience criticism or difficult circumstances may become depressed. We know that health requires more than good nutrition and exercise. Health is wholistic. I once heard Dr. Kenneth Cooper, the aerobics advocate, say: "A person does not die from just one disease, but from his or her whole way of life."

Practice a Balanced Life

A balanced life is like a three-legged stool: physical, emotional, and spiritual. Because it is so basic to wellness, we shall elaborate on *spirituality* first. Historically, a link exists between religious belief and personal health. To avoid falling into "the blues trap," individuals must practice an active, everyday faith in God. Research reveals that at least 96 percent of Americans say they believe in God and try to practice their faith in order to give life meaning.[7]

Harold G. Koenig, founder of the Center for the Study of Spirituality and Medicine at Duke Medical Center, affirms that medical practitioners should take spirituality seriously. He suggests that religious coping can reduce the emotional distress caused by painful life events.

> Patients may "turn over" their problems to God, trusting God to handle them so that they don't have to . . . worry about them. They may believe that God has a purpose in allowing them to experience pain or suffering, which gives suffering meaning and makes it more bearable.[8]

Koenig tells young physicians that their patients may stay well by practicing rituals of their faith, such as prayer, worship, receiving communion, and reading their sacred Scriptures, and by receiving support from clergy or members of their particular faith community.

Research exploring the connection between biology and spiritual practice—once derided as scientific heresy—may offer insight into how persons heal and stay well. Scientific studies have shown that persons who pray regularly and attend religious services stay healthier and live longer than those who rarely or never do—even when age, health, habits, demographics, and other factors are considered. A six-year Duke University study of 4,000 men and women of various faiths, all over age sixty-four, "found that the relative risk of dying was 46 percent lower for those who frequently attended religious services."[9] Dr. Dale Matthews of Georgetown University, author of *The Faith Factor,* notes that some 75 percent of studies of spirituality have confirmed health benefits.[10]

Some scientists speculate that prayer may foster a state of peace and calm that could lead to beneficial changes in the cardiovascular and immune systems, notes investigative reporter Dianne Hales. Using sophisticated brain-imaging techniques, Dr. Andy Newberg of the University of Pennsylvania, author of *Why God Won't Go Away,* has documented changes in blood flow in particular regions of the brain during prayer and meditation. Hales quoted Newberg: "This could be the link between religion and health benefits such as lower blood pressure, slower heart rates, decreased anxiety and an enhanced sense of well-being."[11]

Emotionally, persons who learn to face reality and avoid cognitive distortions may escape what some have termed "the dark night of the soul." Depression is a predictable consequence of thinking/feeling errors in trying to explain things that happen in life. When a person concludes, "It's me. It will always be this way" and then convinces himself or herself that "It has ruined my whole life," he or she is headed for trouble. Psychologist Michael Yapko sees such rationalizations as attributional errors—personalizing things that are *not* personal, assuming things will stay hurtful forever and that they will negatively impact everything that you do.[12]

Physically, you can practice old truths, not simply repeat them. Eat a well-planned, healthy diet; exercise wisely—under medical supervision if that is indicated; remember you have earned the right to rest; get the proper sleep for your situation; and learn to "step outside" stressful relationships and events. Practice problem-solving skills. If you have been a workaholic, learn to play. Invest time and resources in enjoying music, art, travel, sports, drama, reading, and the visual arts.

Select your friends and associates with care. Embrace people you really like, who bring out your best—"such as your sensitivity, sense of humor, playfulness, and affection."[13] In some settings, you may have to change rather than wishing people or situations might change. Socialize with positive—not negative, complaining, mean-spirited—persons. You deserve good people in your life who appreciate you.

Have regular physical, visual, and auditory examinations by competent medical personnel. Certain examinations—such as mammograms for women, prostatic-specific antigen (PSA) verification for men, and colonoscopy examinations—should be obtained on a regular cycle. Life is in the blood; thus, periodic blood tests are essential to determine chemical imbalances and to guide physicians in prescribing correct medications, when necessary. Have essential surgeries when required by accidents, by medical diagnosis of diseased tissue or organs, when orthopedic remedies are indicated, or when pain levels are no longer bearable. At times, it may take a temporary prescription, such as Zoloft or Prozac, to relieve a situational depression.

How Do We Prevent the Blues and the Blahs?

With all that has been suggested in this discussion, you may have already taken positive steps to increase your competency for living. Keeping well is a never-ending calling. These concluding bits of advice are brief and to the point:

- Because we face daily uncertainties, learn to tolerate ambiguity and stress.
- Distinguish realistic from unrealistic expectations; then, attempt the possible.
- Determine events/things you can control and the limits of your responsibility.
- Discern what is true reality from appearances, rumors, gossip, and hearsay.
- Practice integrity in personal/social contexts; then live without regrets.
- Accept your own uniqueness while acknowledging other viewpoints.
- Live in today's real world. Longing for the "good old days" is not a strategy.

A SUMMARY OF KEY POINTS

- You have noted how we focused on positive approaches and encouraging results to retirement challenges. That reasoning explains the inclusion of human interest stories in this consideration of the blues and blahs. Real people in "real-time" situations relied on both human and divine resources, practical wisdom, and courage in escaping the clutches of depression.

- Rather than shallow optimism in addressing this common health issue, we acknowledged that everyone faces adversity. People must face *life,* all kinds of experiences, every day. Causes of depressive responses are complex: biological, social, psychological, and spiritual. Multiple remedies are required to stay well.

- In illustrating the manifold causes and the diagnostic nature of depression, we asked, is it a disease or a disorder? Without describing the abnormal symptoms of clinical depression, which is usually considered a disease, I have featured everyday "blues" or situational depressions as a health disorder. Although religious caregivers may offer both spiritual support and palliative aid in many situations, clinical depression requires medical treatment—counseling, medication, perhaps hospitalization.

- There are numerous strategies for addressing depression and eliminating suicide risk. Staying well is an inside job; yet, it requires preventive skills, attention to the body's complex systems, spiritual coaching, appropriate education, wise counseling, and, when indicated, medically supervised therapies. See psychologist Michael D. Yapko's coaching guide, *Breaking the Patterns of Depression* (Doubleday, 1997) to help eliminate cognitive errors and build expectancy in clients.

Chapter 6

When the Unexpected Happens

The late Carlyle Marney—described variously as a priestly prophet, an ethicist, a preacher's preacher, a brilliant lecturer, and a Christian pilgrim—was a compelling voice for adventurous religion in post-World War II America. Born July 8, 1916, in Harriman, Tennessee, educated in Carson-Newman College and the Southern Baptist Theological Seminary, he served three Kentucky pastorates prior to leading the First Baptist Church, Austin, Texas, from 1948 to 1958. Following nine years as senior minister at Myers Park Baptist Church in Charlotte, North Carolina, Marney established Interpreter's House, an ecumenical center for clergy and laity at Lambuth Inn, Lake Junaluska, North Carolina.

I first encountered this rare man by reading his sermons, *These Things Remain,* published by Abingdon Press in 1953. Postwar America was erupting with change, population growth, advancing technology, and awakening internationalism. Marney examined and expounded biblically on life's enduring values, such as faith, hope, and love. True, his giftedness as a thinker, lecturer, and writer compelled him to publish more books, including *Faith in Conflict, Structures of Prejudice, Priests to Each Other, The Recovery of the Person, The Coming Faith,* and *The Crucible of Redemption: The Meaning of the Cross-Resurrection Event.*

However, it was his first book—*These Things Remain: Thoughts to Live By*—that invited readers to anchor their lives by steadfast faith in God in a swirling sea of change. Marney's apologetic writings were characterized by paradox, like his early companion volume, *Faith in Conflict.* He wisely knew that the unexpected often happens. Then, the only organizing force that can bring order to a trekker's risky journey is faith in a trustworthy Guide. Marney's own life was

Spiritual Wisdom for Successful Retirement
Published by The Haworth Press, Inc. 2006. All rights reserved.
doi:10.1300/5537_07

cut short July 3, 1978, in Lake Junaluska at the age of sixty-one when he died suddenly of a heart attack.

Caregivers who sojourn alongside newly retired persons know that life often takes us where we have not been before. Here, we are considering circumstances, both positive and negative, that may occur when we wander off into unfamiliar territory. How we need guidance for the unseen possibilities in our lives! Clinging fiercely to known persons, structures, and surroundings—*things that remain*—retirees may be ill-prepared for the journey ahead. Thus, we emphasize first the value of being intentional, of planning a steady course in retirement. Then we illustrate approaches for thriving when the unexpected happens and we find ourselves in some wilderness.

THE VALUE OF BEING INTENTIONAL

The Bradfords

Al and Cathy Bradford, a deeply devout couple, envisioned their retirement plans long before Al retired seventeen years ago. He was employed as a machinist in the aircraft manufacturing industry. Because he was already commuting several miles to his workplace, they decided to purchase acreage outside their metropolitan area, build a retirement home, continue to work a few years, and simply extend Al's commute. In the process, their grown children and grandchildren moved to the same new area. Relocating to their new location give Cathy an opportunity to apply for a banking position in a nearby city. They fenced the land and began a secondary career of buying, raising, feeding, and trading cattle.

When the time came for Al to retire, he and Cathy were well-established in their new community and well-connected with friends in a nearby church. Al continued acquiring rural property, trading cattle to build up his herd, and raising and cutting hay for sale. One day, "out of the blue," natural gas was discovered on a close neighbor's ranch. Naturally, agents soon contacted Al and Cathy, and all their neighbors, with offers to lease land for future natural gas exploration. That, along with development of nearby ranchland for home building sites, thrust up the value of their acreage.

The Bradfords had intended a quiet retirement on their ranch, spending some time in travel, but more time in volunteer service, along with enjoying their children and grandchildren. Then the unexpected happened when a windfall came their way that changed everything. Gas well development brought new workers, noisy drilling machinery, and productive gas wells on their land and on their neighbors' adjoining properties. The Bradfords had reasoned that "someday" the leasing companies might develop wells. Now, that hoped-for progress had evolved. Having planned ahead, they felt blessed with their good fortune.

Matters went another way, however, when Al's health deteriorated. He was injured in a fall from his truck while working on the ranch. In time, his back pain was diagnosed as bone cancer. Still, the Bradfords' faith anchored them in the providence of divine care. Like David in biblical times, they faced the future directly within the purpose of God. You may recall stories about Israel's heroic warrior David, reported in 1 Samuel. Anointed to be king as a youth, he was in constant conflict with his predecessor, King Saul—fleeing, fighting, and forgiving. When he became king, he not only defeated Israel's enemies and united a nation, he lusted for Bathsheba and made illicit love with another man's wife—a man whose death he later designed (2 Sam. 11-12, NIV). Despite his sin, openly confessed in Psalms 32 and 51, David tried to respect God in every aspect of his life. Like their biblical heroes, the Bradfords determined to trust God in every aspect of their lives.

The Bridgeses

Intentional retirees look ahead. They survey the terrain: money and health care matters, location and living arrangements, family and friendship ties, medical and transportation resources, tax structures, potential for volunteer activities and recreation, as well as time for serious reflection, worship, and connecting—human and divine. Here is a couple, for instance, who had retired sixteen years earlier and built a retirement home in a carefully designed, gated living community. Their daughter lived about 300 miles away in another state. As they aged in retirement, William and Mary Bridges determined they would not always be able to care for their mountain house and yard. The Bridgeses decided to experiment in a living arrangement near their daughter. They visited their daughter's city, selected an apartment complex near her residence, and rented an apartment for six months.

They wished to experience the new location in a different state, with level not hilly terrain and a warmer climate. While visiting, they had discovered two nursing-type care facilities for frail elderly adults and were invited to lead worship services for the residents of both centers. The Bridgeses elected to experience the potential new living arrangement for six months before selling their mountain cottage and relocating to another state. The temporary move gave them time to become acquainted in the new region, develop medical/dental resources, and connect with persons of similar faith and values. Intentionally, they assessed the cost of living, potential property and state income taxes, educational possibilities, numbers of retirees in the region, as well as recreational resources.

The value of being intentional in retirement planning is recognizing that being retired is a work in progress, with many loose ends, not a marathon. Matters can go another way. Giving up a regular occupation—with all its duties, decisions, and demands—retirees must let go of who they have been. Work has kept them connected and feeling needed all of their adult lives. When retiring, there are farewells, perhaps nice words, and the retiree becomes emeritus (a former employee). With time on one's hands, no longer needed at work, a retiree may feel "out of the loop," cut off from community, and resenting pangs of uselessness.

The noted minister Charles Swindoll wrote in *Growing Strong in the Seasons of Life* of seeing his own father cave in after he retired, as disorientation replaced intentional, decisive living. I quote from his recollection:

> His sense of humor soon lost its keen edge. His once-adventurous spirit turned to restlessness. He talked less, he traveled less, and, what's worse—he *thought* less. Not because he was without money or without health . . . but because he was without purpose. And without close friends. (There was no work schedule, no sense of being needed, a tragic loss of identity.) . . . And it wasn't twelve months before the thief of senility began to steal away the man's drive. Oh, he lived many, many years beyond sixty-five. But most of those years, I'm saddened to say, were marked by tragic disorientation.[1]

He then quoted wisdom from Solomon, about the importance of planning ahead:

> . . . Because childhood and the prime of life are fleeting (Eccles. 11:10, NIV). And because there may be a time when . . . the years draw near when you will say, "I have no pleasure in them." (Eccles, 12:1, NIV)

The Swindoll family's difficult experience further validates the need for intentional living. Not only individuals, nations, and entire cultures can experience the disorienting circumstances of facing the unexpected. It is far from a smooth transition when some unexpected event occurs or threat of an impending tragedy sounds. Any crisis looming on the horizon predictably elevates a nation's feelings of insecurity and anxiety.

LIVING AT LEVEL RED

The air pollution index in this area of north central Texas is symbolized by four codes: green, yellow, orange, and red. During summer days, when temperatures can reach 100 degrees Fahrenheit, an atmospheric inversion often occurs. Given the area's unhealthy ozone level, the weather bureau may issue a "red" unhealthy alert for sensitive groups. Persons allergic to the pollutants may wonder what is making them sneeze and wheeze. Seniors are particularly vulnerable to breathing problems; thus, they are warned to remain indoors during "red" alert days.

More serious issues may arise for lung-impaired patients who have chronic breathing difficulties. When visiting with one such retiree during a "red" alert, I observed the he was dragging a large oxygen tank around as he went about his daily activities. He was short of breath and struggling to breathe. What healthy individuals take for granted—the ability to inhale and exhale deeply—thereby oxygenating their body system, the inhalation therapy patient views as a gift. He faces the constant threat of death. In this case, the patient spoke frankly of life and death issues.

On August 1, 2004, major newspapers across the United States spoke of a much more critical alert—the possibility that terrorists would seek to disrupt the entire U.S. economy. In response, the Homeland Security Secretary raised the terrorism level threat in selected American cities to "orange."[2] Data in the files of an Al Qaeda computer engineer, arrested earlier in Pakistan, led Central Intelligence Agency officials to conclude that terrorists were planning to attack one or several American financial centers. Documentary evidence found after the capture revealed in detail that Al Qaeda operatives had for years conducted extensive reconnaissance of the financial institutions cited in the government's warnings. It is the first terrorism alert for specific sites ever announced in this country.[3]

Living in anticipation that "something terrible might happen" puts many Americans, still terribly shaken following the 9/11 World Trade Center attacks of 2001, on edge. Agreed, no place on earth is completely safe from terrorists; thus, workers in each of the listed Al Qaeda target sites were encouraged to be at work the Monday following the "orange" level alert. In such trying times the best of God's people recognize their need for guidance. They have appreciated the psalmist's affirmation: "For this God is our God forever and ever: he will be our guide even to the end" (Ps. 48:14, NIV). They cling to Christ's pledge to all true believers: "Whoever follows me will never walk in darkness, but will have the light of life" (John 8:12, NIV).

"YOU NEVER KNOW WHAT'S GOING TO HAPPEN"

Here, I shall use *retirement* in a broad sense, for we not only retire at the conclusion of a career but also at numerous endings along life's journey. Put yourself into one or more of the following situations.

- Your flight to Chicago is scheduled for departure at 8:45 a.m. You have packed essential luggage and documents needed for an important appointment the evening before. Arising earlier than usual, you drive through early morning fog and commuter traffic to arrive at an airport parking spot two hours before your scheduled departure. With electronic ticket and boarding pass in hand, you hurriedly make it to the check-in counter only to read the notice "Flight cancelled" by your scheduled flight number.

  "What's gone wrong?" you wonder, running through a mental checklist—mechanical trouble; incoming flight delayed by bad weather; the crew overslept; or what? Checking with the airline personnel, you learn the culprit is a computer glitch. Some 150 flights across the United States have been cancelled; the delays might last for two or three hours, until the system is up and running. You have been inadvertently "retired" from your intended plan to arrive in Chicago on time for your appointment. A passenger standing nearby says disgustedly, "This is inexcusable! So much for technology!"

  Driven Americans do not like to wait. Delays irritate, aggravate; yes, unnerve some people. Impatience can rob the person placed on "hold," by some inadvertence or interference, of his or her good-natured serenity and civility. Religious believers know what the Scriptures tell us: "The fruit of the Spirit is love, joy, peace, patience, kindness, goodness, faithfulness, gentleness, and self-control. Against such things there is no law" (Gal. 5:22-23, NIV). You know such virtues are health-sustaining and life-enhancing; still, a frustrated person may "lose his cool." What is your response to this situation?

- You may identify with the experience of Alice Freeman, who had faced many adversities along life's way—widowed at an early age, compelled to raise two young children while working at a local banking institution, changed occupations during wartime to improve her finances and learn new tasks, and obligated to pay some debts created by her deceased spouse. In order to change her emotional "fortune," Alice determined to go back to school, earn a graduate degree in American history, and seek a college teaching position. With an earned master's degree diploma in hand but no teaching position available in her local college, Alice applied to teach in the local public school system. In time, her dream was realized and she accepted an instructorship in a denominationally owned private college. The next half-decade provided some of the most satisfying professional experiences and rewarding relationships of her life. Popular with students and respected by her faculty colleagues, she determined to work on a doctoral degree at the University of Wisconsin.

Her advanced degree program was well begun in the summers while teaching in the fall and spring semesters. Unfortunately, when a new president was elected by the private college trustees, he determined to replace current master's-level personnel with doctorate-level faculty. Once again, Alice was faced with deep life change when the unexpected happened. At age forty-six, she was obliged to "retire" from teaching and train as a financial investment agent. What is your response?

- Will and Marsha Fleming had enjoyed sixty years of marriage. Growing up and working in the Midwest until his retirement, they had retired to a warmer climate in the southwestern United States. From their earliest years together, they had been homeowners and enjoyed the responsibilities of being in their own house, including the mortgage payments, lawn care, upkeep, and attendant tasks of ownership. They had lived the American dream since World War II.

Now eighty, Will and Marsha had many symptoms of aging and were truly ready to slow down—to give up some responsibilities. They determined to sell their retirement home and rent an apartment in an upscale, multiservice retirement community. They chose the independent living level of care, with the provision that they could elect assisted living or the nursing care facilities, if needed. Recently, a friend asked Will how he and Marsha were adjusting to the new independent living arrangement.

"Marsha likes it fine," he reported. "But I'm having some difficulty adjusting. We've always owned our own place and been free to make our own rules and run our own lives. Now, we live in the Waterford Place apartments, as you know, and there are a hundred rules. I'm not used to being penned up in a small space, with little to do. I miss my woodwork shop and being able to come and go as I please." What if you were in Will's shoes? What is your response?

Numerous changes occur in being *retired* from anything—a delayed airline schedule and missed appointment; dismissal from a satisfying position after long years of struggle to reach a goal; or relinquishment of the freedom and responsibility of home ownership. Can you identify with such frustrating circumstances without feeling defeated? How can religious faith come to your rescue when you face the shattering disappointment of unexpected events? Is your God able to calm your spirit, accompany you in the power of the Holy Spirit, and make a way for you through difficult situations? Perhaps there is a caring person sojourning nearby who models the wisdom and serenity you seek with whom you can share your concerns.

Is it enough to remind yourself that we live in a danger-filled world? The Bible is filled with such warnings. "Do not go out to the fields or walk on the roads, for the enemy has a sword, and there is terror on every side" (Jer. 6:25, NIV). Before sending the sojourners he had called as disciples on mission, Jesus Christ reminded them: "I am sending you out like sheep among wolves . . ." (Matt. 10:16a, NIV). Their first-century Roman-occupied world was alive with soldiers and slaves, with thugs and thieves; thus, anything could happen to God's servants.

WE LIVE IN A DANGER-FILLED WORLD

As they grow older, retired persons tend to become more cautious—about financial matters, about being out on the road after dark, about in taking no unnecessary step. They are cautioned to avoid computer scammers and telephone callers who offer deals that are "too good to be true." The normal wear and tear of life seems difficult enough to manage. Retired persons wish to be courageous in self-care—health, travel, family, and economic matters—but not foolhardy.

Still, close calls come to everyone. Today, the stakes have been raised, and increased risks demand new rules. We are instructed, "Never say *never* because anything may happen at any time." Such warnings seem morbid, however, so we shrug them off until the unimaginable happens. Getting up and beginning a day like any other, we do not dwell on the fragile nature of our human condition. Living one day at a time, the improbable occasionally becomes a self-fulfilling prophecy. Dare we be reminded: we live on an imperiled planet?

Consider some contemporary stories that serve as prisms through which we perceive our violent world.

In October 2002, residents near the nation's capital—from Montgomery County, Maryland, to Fairfax County, Virginia—were frozen in anxiety by the prolonged rampage of two snipers who killed ten persons and wounded three others seriously before being captured. No one knew who might be next.

Late that same month, Russian forces stormed a Moscow theater where hundreds of patrons were being held hostage by Chechen guerillas. Before entering, they introduced a powerful gas into the theater's ventilation and sewer systems, which killed over 100 patrons, along with some forty rebel Chechens. Lyudmila Fedyantseva, who was among the hostages freed by Russian troops, described her feelings during their terror-stricken moments of the attempted rescue. "We dropped to the floor and said good-bye to each other. I was shaking. My mouth was dry. I felt my heart beating."[4] Some 600 Russian and international theatergoers were rushed to area Moscow hospitals, many of them in critical condition.

In Oklahoma that same weekend, a small-town teenager who had been challenged for speeding obtained a gun and shot four neighbors, including a two-year-old girl. He then went on a twenty-mile shooting spree. Two of the random shooter's victims died. How to explain such madness? As though that carnage were not enough for one weekend, a U.S. diplomat was shot dead outside his home in Amman, Jordan. Identified as Lawrence Foley of the U.S. Agency for International Development, he was felled as he walked to his car. None of these victims of violence had any warning; they were slain in a split second of evil, brutal action.

Survivors of episodes of great danger and near-death experiences describe the inner, spiritual change of attitude—akin to conversion—that frequently followed their deliverance. "It's like *seeing* for the first time—all the beautiful people and things I have taken for granted." Or, "I live with new appreciation for each day." Or, "I will tell my children, at least once a day, that I love them." Great sighs of relief for survival are expressed in highly individualistic ways.

Here's an oft-repeated question: "How do people go about living and enduring risks so bravely all of their lives?" What does it take to survive in a danger-filled world? We may find some clues from a Georgia study of ninety-six centenarians (of 36,000 still alive at that time in the United States), reported by Hugh Downs on ABC's *20/20* news-format program.[5] Four characteristics of those survivors showed up repeatedly in the research report.

1. *Optimism:* They were inclined toward hopefulness and confidence. Avoiding shallow Pollyannaism, they lived each day with a positive attitude. It was the German philosopher Wilhelm von Leibniz who espoused the philosophy that this world is the best of all possible worlds. To live hopefully despite everything, one believes that good will ultimately prevail over evil in the universe.
2. *Engagement:* Survivors are involved with other people, absorbed with ideas, and participate in meaningful events. "I keep a full date book," said one retiree. Today, that might mean living with the aid of a PDA or a multitasking picture phone with Internet capability. Engagement implies being occupied, involved, and employed in meaningful activities, not busyness for busyness's sake.
3. *Activity:* Those centenarians interviewed reported participating regularly in some form of physical exercise. Walking was a favorite diversion. Activities ranged from gardening to tutoring, from volunteering with a meals-on-wheels program to an overseas mission-type trip designed to enhance the welfare of faraway people.
4. *Flexibility:* The ability to adapt to loss and change characterized those persons who had endured. In nature, we speak of a plant or tree that can bend in the wind without breaking. Traits like pliable, resilient, and adaptable describe persons who are not wishy-washy but who can grieve losses, let things go, and negotiate transitions that inevitably follow changes.

You may wish to add your own list of traits to optimism, engagement, activity, and flexibility. I believe a profound faith in God is essential to coherent existence in a meaningful Universe. My faith, anchored in the Judeo-Christian scriptures, cherishes reliance on a personal Guide who providentially presides within history. Despite its risks—far from being random chance or luck—life in our Creator's hands is purposeful existence. Caregivers who sojourn alongside you may assist you in viewing life's unexpected events in divine perspective.

CARING MINISTRY
WHEN FACING THE UNEXPECTED

Communities of faith are well-represented in our midst by visionary leaders who inspire mission, speak for God in public ministry, perform worship rituals, and render caring ministries among God's people. Pastoral caregivers are called to provide listening love and spiritual resources for persons facing life's unexpected events. I have suggested that as persons turn to *being* rather than *doing* tasks, and live in the in-between time, they still have great value. Retirees may no longer be productive in the world of work, but they are full-time human beings, created in the image of God. Ministers and trained congregational leaders are called to cherish retired persons by being present with them, listening to their stories, sharing their faith journeys, and encouraging hope in God. They have a past and a future.

In Chapter 5, I suggested that we are our stories. Older persons enjoy recalling earlier life events and telling their stories. In retirement, they may have assembled numerous photo albums, audio or video recordings of pivotal events in their past, along with records of travels, correspondence, and prized memorabilia. Life review—along with symbols such as art, jewelry, books, prized letters, and "stuff" they have collected—characterizes this phase of life. People who are able to look back and recall key events, dear family members and friends, and nodal historical dates enjoy sharing them with attentive listeners.

Events that once seemed like multicolored threads of achievement and failure, of joy and sorrow, birth and death, attachment and detachment have now become the tapestry of a life story. Many seniors "can recall times when God's providence was manifested, and remembering God's strength in difficult times can affirm that God will continue the divine activity until the last."[6] What people remember and share reveals their identities. The storyteller who relates tales of travels, reports professional achievements, or brags on his or her grandchildren's accomplishments is not merely imparting information. She or he is telling the listener *who* she or he is. Caregivers who show interest in retired seniors' stories are actually affirming their worth while encouraging future stories in this important stage of life.

Sarah A. Butler is Canon Pastor of St. John's Episcopal Cathedral in Denver, Colorado, where she has supervised the congregation's caring ministries for many years. She provides wise counsel, educational seminars, and resource referrals for senior adults, "Wisdom People," as she prefers to call them. She has suggested some practical strategies for ministry that I shall paraphrase here.[7]

- Treat older persons as peers who deserve respect. Talking down to retirees, who may have some physical limitations or memory loss, is inappropriate. They are not children, but persons who need to share their experiences, express their faith, and make wise choices, even small ones. They need the resources of the Christian faith.
- Be clear about what you will or will not do for them. Someone once said, "The promises we make can keep us awake. The promises we keep permit us to sleep." Do what you tell a retiree you will do, but do not overpromise to run errands, make calls, deliver messages, read mail, etc. If you are not prepared to assist someone with a matter, you may have to refer that person to an appropriate source of help.
- Approach difficult subjects as adult with adult, respecting the person's integrity and privacy. Lonely adults sometime mention difficult subjects such as their own death or guilt over past failures. Family failures are particularly difficult to reveal and accept. Regard each loss or disappointment seriously and compassionately. Such times of deep sharing are sacred moments. You are on holy ground.
- Accept the fact that retirees can change and grow. They not only have a past; they have today and tomorrow. Encourage them to think of the future. Their future stories may give them a reason to live, so hear them well. Yes, checkmate any unreasonable idea, but affirm their attempts to move forward with life.

Not every caregiver will be called on to minister to the older generation, notes Butler. We should remember that losses, gains, and crises may occur at any life stage. Earlier, I illustrated that retirements come to persons in increments, not in torrents. Caregivers can "be there" for persons who desire to share their story at any age. We are works in progress, being formed, by divine grace, into what we shall become.

A SUMMARY OF KEY POINTS

- Life for retirees is often experienced as a series of paradoxes. What is supposed to work out a certain way does not happen as one had anticipated. As Carlyle Marney wrote a generation ago, our most profound religious faith may experience conflict and contradiction, but that is no reason to give up.
- Intentionality does not lead people astray. Rather, facing life with purpose offers a chart and compass for life's turbulent journey. Just because someone wants something to be so does not make it happen. One must aim for it. Failure to dream can be deadly.
- We never know what a day will bring forth. Warnings of a day with level *orange* regarding national security or level *red* for atmospheric conditions is meant to save lives. After 9/11 the world can no longer go about business as usual.
- With crises looming on the earth, you never know what is going to happen. So, it is best to place your faith in God and reliable human guides, not in technology alone. Retirees who practice optimism, remain engaged, stay active, and are flexible have built-in survival gear for life's journey.
- Retirees are works in progress, being formed into God's individual works of art. Caregivers who walk alongside seniors as sojourners are to respect them for their worth as created in the divine image and to listen well to their stories. They are more than the sum of their past histories; they are also part of God's future.

Chapter 7

There Is Strength in Numbers

The circle of clay figures was displayed on a table laden with unusual crafts from two hemispheres. The art piece featured seven human forms, standing embraced on a platform, with a candle in the center. The Santa Fe shop owner where we found the symbol of *life together* was a native of Guatemala. Instantly smiling, attentive, and accommodating, the woman's brown skin added warmth to her well-stocked curio shop. It was the huge red pepper arrangements hanging near the entrance that first caught my eye, but it was the wealth of woven goods, variety of imported art and craft pieces, home furnishings, and colorful Mexican pottery that captivated our interest.

Because my wife and I were driving, we had space in our vehicle for a few collectibles during the New Mexico vacation. The red-brown cluster of seven supporting figures suggested the presence of companions. Because art's meaning, like beauty, resides in "the eye of the beholder," to us the piece symbolized mutual support, group strength, and team effort in performing our societal responsibilities. The symbol of linkage within the human family reminded us of poet John Donne's memorable lines: "No man is an Iland, intire of it selfe; every man is a peece of the Continent, a part of the maine. . . . any mans [sic] death diminishes me, because I am involved in Mankinde."[1] The artistic figures epitomized the ancient truth that "two are better than one. . . . If one falls down, his friend can help him up" (Eccles. 4:9-10, NIV). Today, the keepsake is displayed prominently in our family room.

Persons planning retirement often look at the process in isolation, as their own private purview of potential outcomes and pitfalls. They do not discuss their plans with other family members, including their adult children—and sometimes their spouses. Because retirement connotes the possibility that one might be considered "over the hill"

Spiritual Wisdom for Successful Retirement
Published by The Haworth Press, Inc. 2006. All rights reserved.
doi:10.1300/5537_08

or "out of the loop," some reticent retirees keep their plans to themselves. That is a big mistake. Retirees need other people!

Imagine the value of amassed strength in times of war. We are told the quadrennial Olympic Games draw thousands of athletes from over 200 nations, plus promoters, security forces, and countless TV viewers. When disasters, such as hurricanes and forest fires strike, the American Red Cross and Federal Emergency Management Agency (FEMA) mobilize relief teams to aid victims. Individuals, standing alone, would be helpless to face crises like Hurricane Katrina's losses.

With the need for each other in mind, we shall look at the significance of family ties and the power of relationships. After all, the need for acceptance, respect, and companionship continues all of our lives. Awareness of "the others" increases when one gives up daily relationships in the workplace, experiences isolation from meaningful associates, and reconsiders life's larger societal responsibilities.

SHARING AN INTERPERSONAL WORLD

How It All Begins

With every child's birth the human race begins anew. Although I do not mean that the human race literally starts with one child's birth, an infant does begin the journey of becoming a fully human, mature individual. In a culture where childlessness is stylish, even popular, among career-oriented couples, delayed parenthood is common. Accepting the God-given assignment of continuing the divine creation is a couple's pathway to parenthood. Parenting is the critical skill essential to establishing each child as a healthy, informed, functional member of society. Many persons who are biologically able to enjoy sex, copulate, and reproduce young are ill-equipped to perform the fundamental and costly responsibilities of parenting.

Given a desire for a child, we might imagine the excitement of a couple sharing the good news of *her* pregnancy and *their* expectancy. Couples who are physically unable to accomplish conception may go to enormous lengths to generate a new being between them. Cost of medical intervention and in-utero implantation of a fertilized egg is exceedingly expensive. Even then, gynecologists report only a 30 percent success rate for placental attachment and fetal development in the uterus. Infertile couples who despair of natural offspring often elect to adopt children, many of whom come from countries such as Russia, China, Vietnam, and Romania.

Creating and sustaining the life of a little child involves much more than doing what comes naturally. It entails participation in a unique family history and education in the lore of a particular tribal, cultural, and national group. A new life begins in almost total helplessness and dependency on environing persons. To raise a child is to meet its need for belonging to a particular family's stories, legends, and rituals. Yet, in order to become a real person, the child must develop a *story* of his or her own. Identifying with the language and lore of one's people imprints the growing child with his or her unique identity.

Bonding and Self-Differentation

To enjoy and share an interpersonal world, we relate with other persons throughout the entire life cycle. We are the sum of our attachments, especially early family relationships and their expressions throughout a lifetime. Through music, Barbra Streisand made famous the phrase, "People who need people are the luckiest people in the world." The British psychoanalyst John Bowlby (1907-1990) spent a lifetime investigating the significance of attachments and their disruption through loss, with consequent grief work.

The son of a surgeon father, Bowlby studied at the University of Cambridge where, by his third year, he became interested in developmental psychology. Following years of direct observation of children's familial relationships at the famed Tavistok Clinic, and elsewhere, he recorded findings concerning separation, loss, and grief. Bowlby held that no influences have more far-reaching effects on personality development than a child's experiences within the family.[2] A Freudian revisionist, he saw a secure base in parent-child relations as the keystone to healthy human development.

Enabling adults—parents and teachers, along with siblings, peers, artists, politicians, representatives of the media, ministers, priests and rabbis, athletes, entertainers, public safety officers, and, yes, child welfare agents, even the judiciary—invest growing youths with resources to develop into maturity. At any point along the way, the developing child may veer off course—under negative influences of violent video games, Internet chat rooms, or the seductions of addictive behaviors. To achieve healthy selfhood in his or her own time, a child must learn to walk, then to walk away from parenting figures. The faithful parent figure lets go of each child in such a way that dependency may be transcended and friendships formed for the journey of faith together under God.

According to basic tenets of Bowlby's findings, retirees who face life unafraid function from an internal base of emotional and spiritual security. They are at home in their own skin, know who they are, what life's boundaries consist of, and are able to relate freely and responsibly with other persons throughout a lifetime.

Unfortunately, millions of children and youth experience cutoffs from family identification, solidarity, and stability. Children born into blended families often form a third tier of offspring. After *his* and *hers,* there are *ours.* Some youngsters fit well into stepparenting arrangements; others fall through the cracks because of sibling rivalry, parental jealousy, favoritism, abuse, or rejection. There are now 20 million mixed marriages in America. Their offspring often identify with one or the other parent, but not with both. Physical features, language differences, cultural and religious values, and customs differ between parents, and their behaviors may be flawed as models for identification. Adopted children are often told they are special as *chosen* family members but may spend a lifetime searching for their "real" birth parents. Add to these numbers children born with physical or mental challenges, millions of offspring of AIDS-infected parents who are destined to die prematurely, along with runaways and addicts who end up in gangs, halfway houses, and prisons.

As adults, their pathways are littered with the debris of fractured families, abuse, neglect, poverty, gang violence, institutionalization, and conflicts with educators, law enforcers, welfare authorities, and members of the judicial system. We need healthy, caring persons to function as surrogate parents for wounded youth, and we need trustworthy *bridge parent* figures—relatives, teachers, coaches, ministers, friends—to support hurting youth and provide healthy models.

Spiritual Nurture of Family Strength

You may be reflecting on your own early upbringing, recalling people who meant much to you while growing up: ideal parent figures or favorite teachers and friends. How are we made strong through healthy family identification? Ideally:

- A wholesome family gives each child a name by which he or she is known throughout the life span. Whether or not you like your given name, nickname, or surname, you have had many opportunities to put meaning into your name.
- Healthy parents provide room, psychic space, and safe places— an environment in which children blossom and grow. Looking back, did your family accept and affirm you, treat you with fairness and justice, and provide you a *voice* in the family circle? Was there always a place at the table for you? If yes, you were blessed.
- Wise parents educate (from the Latin, *educare*—"to lead out") each child in the language, lore, religious faith, and values of their particular family, tribe, nation, and culture. Self-esteem is the treasured by-product of such family preparation.
- Spiritual sojourners free children to grow from dependence on powerful providers, through the independence of adolescent years, to interdependent relationships in adulthood. You are fortunate if your support community blessed you and stood with you as you established yourself in the adult powerfield.
- The healthy adult is ready to marry and establish a home of his or her own.

STRENGTHS OF AN ENDURING MARRIAGE

Marriage Changes Things

Thoughts of marriage for young lovers conjure up images of waiting breathlessly at some altar for the wedding ceremony to end and the celebrating to begin. The pair is lost in themselves. Yet, the divine directive for marriage partners confirms their linkage with and indebtedness to their families of origin. "For this reason [i.e., marriage] a man will leave his father and mother and be united to his wife, and they will become one flesh" (Gen. 2:24, NIV). A wedding's intent is to ritualize the leaving and cleaving process in which a couple both honor their pasts and begin life together with God's blessing.

In retrospect, a retired couple may reflect on the paradoxical process of separating from their parents and becoming connected as covenant partners. Rather than private living arrangements, relationships, possessions, schedules, and obligations, the married couple blends into a new social identity. More than name, address, banking, and credit card changes are involved. The romantic, playful, and erotic games of prewedding rituals must give way to more serious tasks of forging lasting bonds in marriage. As "joint heirs of the grace of life," they will discover that love is not an event but a lifelong process (1 Peter 3:7b, NIV).

What may have taken a man or woman years to achieve in differentiating from parents is now submerged in the depths of body and soul bonding. New rhythms must be worked out with due regard for individual differences and the need for negotiating preferences in self-care, timing, territoriality, lovemaking, and health matters; tending relationships; managing work schedules; facing struggles; and assuming the economies of practical homemaking tasks.

Retirees understand that marriage partners should be free to pursue individual centers of interest and to use their different gifts and skills within the marital economy. The wife, for example, may enjoy shopping, gardening, and reading romantic novels and favor Oriental décor; while her husband might prefer sporting events and enjoy computer time and listening to country and western music. "Most couples can remember how struggles in the early years forged a closeness between them. Unfortunately, however, the bonds that hardships foster do not always endure when conditions improve," note ministers Herbert Anderson and Robert Cotton Fite. "If the bonding is *only* a by-product of struggle [or of selfish sexual games], it is likely to diminish when the conditions change that prompted the emotional bond in the first instance."[3]

The Seasons of Marriage

In a tribute to his wife, Barbara, after thirty-five years of marriage, noted author Calvin Miller wrote: "Old promises must pledge themselves each day; or, unrenewed, pass quietly away."[4] Miller's *A Covenant for All Seasons* affirms the fragility and delicacy of marriage as it develops into "a mature love that is for better, for worse, for always."

The expectations that cause a maturing couple the most difficulty are those that are unclear at the outset, held secret, or altered over time. A spouse may not recognize why she is unhappy with the man she married. She simply feels manipulated, unfulfilled, taken advantage of, unappreciated, or sinned against in the relationship. The marriage is not what she had hoped for. A man, on the other hand, may feel rejected or short-changed in the bedroom and fantasize about a fresh, exciting romance. Infidelities begin, not with one's anatomy, but in the human heart as a person's loves are corrupted by jealousy, anger, abuse, injustice, illness, or conflict.

Marriages not only change things and people, they form their own identities and change over time. Ideally, the retirees' life together is not merely endurable but enjoyable. You and your spouse are fortunate if you are still sweethearts, attend to each other's needs, hold each other in high regard, and practice a fair balance of power and control. For many retired persons, losses through divorce or death have already occurred. One's soul mate and lover is gone. Having been single before marriage; you may become single again and must perform all the tasks and assume all the responsibilities of a single householder.

The seasons of marriage usher us through the ecstasies of conjugal love *(eros)*, the changing circumstances of lifelong companionship *(philia)*, to enduring commitments of care and compassion *(agape)*.[5] Here, C. S. Lewis makes a helpful distinction between gift-love and need-love. "Divine Love is Gift-love," wrote Lewis. "Need-love cries to God from our poverty; Gift-love longs to serve, or even to suffer for, God." In applying these distinctions to marriage, Lewis noted that "Need-love says of a woman 'I cannot live without her'; Gift-love longs to give her happiness, comfort, protection—if possible, wealth. . . ."[6] We especially think of his loving relationship with his wife, Joy Davidman, who preceded Lewis in death.

The romantic poetess Elizabeth Barrett Browning (1806-1861) poignantly expressed love's full measure of devotion in these memorable lines excerpted from "Sonnets from the Portuguese."

> How do I love thee? Let me count the ways.
> I love thee to the depth and breadth and height
> My soul can reach, when feeling out of sight
> For the ends of Being and ideal Grace. . . .

I love thee with a love I seemed to lose
With my lost saints,—I love thee with the breath,
Smiles, tears, of all my life!—and, if God choose,
I shall but love thee better after death.

As long as life together lasts, the bonds of your marriage covenant form strong cords binding you to God and to your life partner.

Contemplating Care for Marriage Partners

Not everyone will be called on to minister to married persons, especially to retired and older couples. Think of your own marriage as you consider what couples may face at any age. Here are some guidelines to keep in mind.

- The bond between *male* and *female*, established by the Creator (see Gen. 1:27; 2:18, NIV), forms the basis for an enduring friendship and reveals the mutual dependency that characterizes marriage. Persons are strengthened and fulfilled by the unconditional acceptance, love, and support of a member of the opposite sex who complements their personalities and shares life's challenging journey.
- Companions (from the Latin *companis*—"with bread") who commit to respect, cherish, provide for, and remain loyal to each other for life form a unique union. The biblical ideal is one man and one woman together for life—an exclusive, durable physical, emotional, and spiritual relationship.
- As "the two become one," each partner retains his or her own unique selfhood while enfolding the other in a delicate dance of belonging. The relationship is like one ocean touching two shores while respecting each shore's autonomy. The goal of belonging is sharing, not symbiosis, supporting each other while freeing each other to become all he or she can be.
- Marriage affords companions strength to perform the demanding tasks of a legal, mystical, social relationship while sharing reciprocity of responsibility.
- There is always the risk of getting hurt because of the different genders and temperaments of those who choose to link life together. Couples who walk the same path seek justice (fair

play/fair power) for each other and offer forgiveness and recon-
ciliation to each other when in error.
- To have a healthy marriage, couples should be candid, honest,
  and vulnerable with each other. Their relationship must be an
  open system—transparent before God and, at the same time,
  open to significant *others* on their earthly journey.

THE GIFT OF FRIENDSHIP

Having experienced an enjoyable, restorative vacation as guests of
a friend in North Carolina, for my wife and I find it hard to imagine
what unbefriended life is like. To build a better world, we need
friends yet not necessarily persons of our own resolve. Special people
come into our lives by choice but also through the grace and generosity of God and through referrals by other friends. Let us reflect on
some of the benefits from the gift of authentic friendship.

Americans are often glib about friendliness. Once on a plane, I sat
by a man from Miami. He was on a "first name" basis in an instant;
then, he offered to buy me an alcoholic drink (which I declined). He
was the type of person who never really lets you *inside* where the real
person lives. Friendship for many people is a commodity rather than
what William Penn, founder of the Pennsylvania Quaker colony,
called "a union of spirits" and "a marriage of hearts." A genuine
friend is someone you trust, with whom you can share your heart—
your true self.

Many kinds of friends fill our distracted lives: our spouses, neighbors, generous friends, status-and-using people, and intergenerational friends. We have exbusiness associates, special-occasion companions, far-away buddies, professional allies, soul friends, and lifelong
comrades. For Christian believers there is the transforming friendship
of Jesus Christ. A true friend is a person who knows us well, with
whom we risk transparency, vulnerability, perhaps hurt. A dependable friend seeks our best welfare, listens to our stories, and tends to
our heartaches and concerns. Soul friends pray for and with us; inter-
pret us to folks who criticize or fail to understand us; challenge us
when we falter; and stand by us with fidelity, integrity, and courage
on life's journey.

Levels of Friendship

Spontaneous friends surprise us with their acceptance, availability, and affirmation. We experience their acceptance as generosity, their availability as companionship, and their affirmation as strength.

You may have known *status-and-using friends* who latch onto others on a need-love basis. Because they are seeking favors or enablement, we experience their presence as manipulative and their contacts as exploitive. The university freshman girl who suddenly becomes the object of some jock's attention may end a social event as a date rape case rather than with a happy story for her friends. Status-and-using persons usurp our time, deplete our resources, test our patience, and may mobilize our hostility.

Life-stage friends pass through our lives in each developmental transition. Two- to five-year-old playmates may enjoy and keep one another company but disappear during school-age years. Chumship often develops between same-sex youngsters through about ages ten to twelve. Adolescent friends come in many shapes and sizes—fickle, high achievers, sports buddies, also hurtful persons.

Coming-of-age adult friends are in the same boat of struggles for success, job search, mate selection, and gaining a firm foothold in the adult powerfield. Cost-of-living arrangements and expenses are often pooled. Intimacy at this stage may not evolve into marriage, but every successful love experience strengthens one's capacity to love.

Lifelong *adult friendships* may emerge through contacts in educational or occupational settings; during military service; or sharing common experiences such as travel, working out in a health club, experiencing illness or divorce; enjoying a hobby; or vacationing with the same tour group. Retirement communities provide occasions for meeting new persons: as neighbors, at meals, in worship or Bible study, at game tables, sharing hobbies (e.g., golf or tennis), in book review clubs, or by participating in travel experiences.

Soul friends bond at the deepest, most intimate level of friendship. One's spouse, ideally, is one's best friend. Enduring relationships may not only be experienced between persons who have things in common. In physics, opposites attract; this may also hold true with one's companions. Symbolically, soul friends have "been through the war" together. Shoulder to shoulder, they have been on paths that are dangerous and real. They understand each other and, at the deepest level, meet each other's needs. Such friendships, forged over time, are both rare and real.

THE BIBLE AND FRIENDSHIP

You might select other stories than the following examples, but these references stand out. Think of David, whom Samuel anointed to become king, and Jonathan, son of Israel's reigning King Saul. Because of their ages and shared experiences in peacetime and war, "Jonathan became one in spirit with David, and he loved him as himself," i.e., as his own soul (1 Samuel 18:1, NIV). Once, when David was hiding from Saul, who had vowed to take his life, "Saul's son Jonathan went to David at Horesh and helped him find strength in God. 'Don't be afraid,' he said. 'My father Saul will not lay a hand on you. You will be king over Israel, and I will be second to you. Even my father knows this'" (1 Samuel 23:16-17, NIV).

Horesh was the last recorded meeting between Jonathan and David. Jonathan's friendship and respect for David enabled him to accept a subordinate role to David without any sign of jealousy or resentment.

Another Old Testament model of friendship is that of Ruth, a Moabitess daughter-in-law, and Naomi, a Jewish woman. Their friendship spanned a generation and national boundaries. To frame the story, Naomi and her husband, Elimelech, moved from Judah to Moab with their two sons, who later married. With the passing of time, all three men died. Widowed Naomi planned a return to Judah. She urged her daughters-in-law, Orpah and Ruth, to return to their homeland, and Orpah obeyed.

Then, the story changes. "But Ruth replied, 'Don't urge me to leave you or to turn back from you. Where you go I will go, and where you stay I will stay. Your people will be my people and your God my God. Where you die I will die, and there I will be buried'" (Ruth 1:16-17, NIV). Naomi became convinced that Ruth was determined to go home with her; thus, she accepted Ruth's affirmation of loyalty.

There are many references to friendship in the Scriptures. On one occasion, Jesus freely chose to call his disciples friends (John 15:15, NIV). It is said that Jesus loved Martha and her sister and Lazarus, companions in the city of Bethany (John 11:5, NIV). The writer of

Acts relates events surrounding the friendship of Barnabas to Paul the apostle (Acts 9:17, NIV). Paul was befriended in his travels and determination to visit Rome. His friend, Luke, wrote of greeters who welcomed the travelers on their way.

"On seeing them Paul thanked God and took courage" (Acts 28:15, NIV). Paul mentored young missioners Titus and Timothy and was their teacher. Romans 16 (NIV) lists Paul's personal greetings to a multitude of fellow workers by name. And in his letter to the church at Philippi, Paul mentioned friends, including "those who belong to Caesar's household" (Phil. 4:22, NIV).

Empowered in the Strength of Friends

On the subject of the empowerment that may come to us from friends, let us consider some things that friendship may accomplish.

- Friends encourage the humanizing process. They validate the worth of human personality, confirm the continuity of life, and inspire us on the journey of faith. They visit us when we are ill and seek to comfort us in our sorrows. In some cases, close friends share great "dangers, toils, and snares," even to the point of death, and then try to keep the cherished person's memory alive. Consider this example.

    Some years ago, Gloria and I shared an American Summer Institutes study experience in Leysin, Switzerland. A highlight for us was meeting Renate and Eberhard Bethge, a niece of Dietrich Bonhoeffer and her husband. A founder of Germany's Confessing Church during World War II, Bonhoeffer became a Nazi prisoner and was martyred at Flossenburg Prison April 9, 1945. Renate related how she and other family members prayed for Dietrich and took him food items and small gifts during his several 1943-1945 prison experiences. Eberhard collected many of Dietrich's writings and published them under titles such as *Ethics* (1949) and *Letters and Papers from Prison* (1953). Bethge, who died on March 18, 2000, wrote a biography of Bonhoeffer, first published in 1957.[7]
- True friends fill vacuums created by earlier failed relationships, compensate for profound losses, and offer us spiritual nurture on the journey. They seek to soften psychic wounds inflicted by others and help us correct mistakes we have made along the way.

Having personally experienced difficult family losses in the past, I was encouraged by this note that once came from a treasured friend: "Thank you for the tie that binds our hearts in Christian love." Such friends are angels unaware!

- Cherished friends call up the best part of ourselves. Although they know our darker sides, they accept us as we are. You do not have to fight for a place with people you prize. You always have a place—in their hearts, minds, calendars, and prayers. When next you meet, you simply take up where you left off with the last visit, e-mail message, or conversation. Gloria and I display pictures of family and friends in our kitchen so we have daily reminders of their companionship.

- When we feel marginalized or less appreciated than other persons, good friends help us overcome feelings of "differentness" or of being overlooked. For example, although I had studied with other good teachers on different campuses than had he, a respected colleague in another institution affirmed my acceptance into a coveted professional guild. His encouraging note read simply, "You are *in*!" It felt good.

You should never underestimate the power of your actions with other people. With one small gesture you can change a person's life for better or for worse. More than private individuals, however, are involved. A courageous, wise leader can change the fortunes of a multinational corporation or of a key educational institution. One candidate for public office might lift a community to a new level of justice for its citizens. With one act of courage an entire nation might be saved from environmental ruin, a terrorist attack, or a nuclear disaster. The positive influence of one person often enhances the strength of many others.

A SUMMARY OF KEY POINTS

- Sojourners who share the interpersonal journey with fellow pilgrims have a larger assignment than they initially imagine. Caregivers must attend to *both* a person throughout his or her life span *and* the shaping matrix—family, tribe, community, or national culture in which he or she is embedded.

- Once they become alert to life's systemic webs and to the stages along life's way, wise caregivers will address human complexities in a real-time world. Fragile elderly friends, for example, require an entirely different understanding of human development issues than, say, a newlywed couple. Wise ministry is age-appropriate.
- Preparation for marriage is a lifetime concern. People change, and love changes. Deep covenants help hold partners together when romantic love no longer prevails. Yet commitments often collide, and people break their promises. Thus, "old promises must pledge themselves each day; or, unrenewed, pass quietly away."
- Authentic friendship is a treasured gift. No matter one's age or life stage, we need other people. Remember, life is not easy for an older single person. Practice ways to express your interest in persons. Risk reaching out to strangers. Dare being honest with people you trust and nurture relationships that matter.
- Contemplate a pivotal experience in your own life in which the "power of friendship" helped you discern a course of direction or receive strength for some difficult task. Then, consider your fellow strugglers who may need your friendship.

Chapter 8

Facing Death and the Life Beyond

Death comes. Sooner or later each of us will experience the transition from this life to the next. Death's stark reality was pictured in the classic World War II film *From Here to Eternity*. A tale of romance and the tragic interruptions of war, the plot locates action at Schofield in Hawaii and reveals how the Japanese attack on Pearl Harbor, December 7, 1941, changed each character's life. All the connections that held their sources of meaning together were disrupted amid deaths and career changes.

The film depicts how the impartial forces of war collide with the individual destinies of people, throwing them into turmoil, separation, and death. War, like international terrorism, is bigger than individual losses.[1] In the Iraqi war, we recall that countless American troops and hapless civilians died. Scars of war—along with accidents, diseases, tragic incidents, and homicides—are daily reminders of life's fragility. The smell of death pervades our senses from the cradle to the grave. Still, you may deny that, someday, people will view your body and repeat the cliché, "Doesn't he [she] look natural?"

We hold positive images of dying as well. Once, in Cape Town, South Africa, Gloria and I visited the cardiac surgery suite of Groote Schuur Hospital where Dr. Christiaan N. Barnard had performed the world's first human heart transplant. With doctorates from both the University of Cape Town and the University of Minnesota, the soon-to-be famous Chris Barnard introduced to the world a significant way to prolong life. Barnard's December 3, 1967, feat, performed on a fifty-seven-year-old grocer named Louis Washkansky, was made possible by the accidental death of twenty-five-year-old Denise Ann Darvall. She had stepped into the path of an oncoming vehicle while leaving a doughnut shop and was critically injured. At death, her parents agreed to donate her heart to make the transplant surgery possi-

Spiritual Wisdom for Successful Retirement
Published by The Haworth Press, Inc. 2006. All rights reserved.
doi:10.1300/5537_09

ble. Although Washkansky died of pneumonia after eighteen days, he lived long enough to tell his story, recorded in *To the Last Heartbeat*.[2]

By all means, we desperately hold on to life. Leigh Bills, frantic for a human donor's gift for her four-month-old son, who needed a heart, confessed: "It is getting harder and harder to hope. I feel stranded in sadness and the only way out is the tragic gift of a stranger."[3] Because only an infant's vital organ would suffice, she turned to a specialist in Berlin, Germany, who had helped develop a mechanical heart to save newborns' lives. Although humankind has long sought to hold death at bay—to prolong life—we know each of us is "destined to die once, and after that to face judgment" (Heb. 9:27, NIV).

Throughout history people have sought means with which to extend life and delay death. A ninety-year-old mother—with cancer of the colon, bladder, and ovary—finally yielded to her children's insistence that she have surgery. Afterward, her surgeon reported, thankfully, that the tumor had not spread to other parts of her body. Such positive outcomes encourage us to defy the ravages of disease through medical science or by other means. The following inquiry into aspects of death and the life beyond will permit us to engage the subject further and examine the complex interfaces of time and eternity.

PHILOSOPHICAL AND LITERARY PERSPECTIVES

Americans are products of the humanist-religious strands of Western thought, found in the writings of early philosophers such as Socrates, Plato, and Aristotle and modern existentialists like Martin Heidegger and Jean-Paul Sartre. Most of them struggled with the ominous fact that death is the end of life. No where is this being/nonbeing anxiety more clearly stated than in philosophical theologian Paul Tillich's *The Courage to Be*. The courage to face one's death anxiety, held Tillich, resides in the confidence of our "being accepted into communion with God . . . , not a questionable theory of immortality. . . . Encountering God means encountering transcendent security and transcendent eternity."[4] In order for one to participate in God, thereby sharing in God's eternal nature, Tillich held that we must accept God's acceptance of us.

An ancient sage reflected reverent agnosticism about death and the life beyond. He wrote simply that the Creator has "set eternity in the hearts of men" (Eccles. 3:11, NIV). The Greek philosopher Socrates (469?-399 BC) understood this fact. He left no writings, but his philosophy is known through the works of his pupil Plato. Officials in Athens condemned Socrates to death for his unconventional teachings. *Plato's Apology* recorded Socrates' reflections on dying before he drank a cup of hemlock and lay down on his couch to die. "It is now time to depart,—for me to die, for you to live. But which of us is going to a better state is unknown to every one but God."

Early in the twentieth century, German existentialist Martin Heidegger noted the importance of viewing life in the light of death in his germinal work, *Sein und Zeit (Being and Time).*[5] Mundane events and cares of life, noted Heidegger, trap humankind in inauthentic existence. Only as a person considers the trivial concerns, crises, and preoccupations of everyday experience in the light of death's certainty may one achieve authentic existence. His eschatological understanding of life as "being toward death" lacks the reassurance of the Christian faith's promise of eternal life through the life, death, and resurrection of Jesus Christ (see NIV, Rom. 8:18-30; 1 Cor. 15:20-58; Gal. 3:29; James 2:5; Titus 3:7).

Along with our own experiences of grief and loss, we have been influenced by the observations of writers such as C. S. Lewis, whose wife's death prompted his reflections in *A Grief Observed.*[6] While studying at Oxford University, Sheldon and Davy Vanauken were drawn to the Christian faith, in part, by reading Lewis's writings and corresponding with the Oxford don. Vanauken and his beloved Davy (from her surname Jean Davis) became two of Lewis's favorite confidants. In *A Severe Mercy,* Vanauken's tribute to their love and life together, the Virginia professor detailed the events surrounding Davy's lingering, and finally fatal, illness.[7] Her liver was damaged, doctors concluded, by a viral infection that prematurely ended her life in a Charlottesville, Virginia, hospital.

The day after Davy's death, a small box containing her ashes was handed to the grieving Vanauken. He drove to the St. Stephen's church cemetery. As snowflakes drifted down, he reported kneeling by a stone cross and praying while holding the box and a rose. To quote his words:

It was cold—the dead of winter. I opened the box and began to scatter the ashes, using a sower's motion. When I had done, the flakes were coming down hard. I left the rose on the old cross. I said aloud: "Go under the Mercy". . . . Her ashes were [soon] covered with the blanket of snow.[8]

The ways of death, grieving, adapting to the emptiness, and imagining what life is like beyond what Leslie Weatherhead called "that immortal sea" lie in the fallow fields of our individual imaginations. The poet James Whitcomb Riley expressed his search for a solution as "dreaming how very fair [heaven] needs must be." He wrote:

> I cannot say, and I will not say
> That he is dead. He is just away.
> With a cheery smile, and a wave of the hand,
> He has wandered into an unknown land.[9]

Dying persons wander "into an unknown land" in many ways—from lingering illness to instant death by accident or self-inflicted wound, from fatal diseases like AIDS to the wasteland of degenerative neurological disorders like Alzheimer's, from stillbirth to annihilation by war or earthquake. Our lingering questions about death and the life beyond are best understood as we continue to pursue a multidimensional perspective.

A BIOLOGICAL/CLINICAL PERSPECTIVE

Death may be figurative, as in the comment, "His death occurred when he retired, although he still lived for years." There are numerous references to spiritual death in the Hebrew-Christian Scriptures, none more sobering than "the wages of sin is death" (Rom. 6:23, NIV). We speak of the death of one's dream, the ending of a relationship, and youth's loss of innocence. Novelist George Eliot noted that in every parting there is an image of death. Any ending may be like dying: the accidental loss of a limb, bankruptcy of a corporate entity, or letting go of who we were. If one feels shame for being helplessly trapped in the web of chemical dependency, something dies in that person's soul.

The ending of any form of life in persons, animals, or plants is both physical and final. Or is it? Defining death has become more complicated because of advances in medical technology. When the human heart ceases to beat, breathing stops, and brain waves stop, we speak of that person as being dead. Today, however, doctors can artificially prolong the working of the human heart and lungs. Machines can maintain a heartbeat and breathing in a person who, otherwise, might be considered deceased.

So, when is a person legally dead? Most states in the United States have adopted the Uniform Determination of Death Act of 1980. "Under this act, a person is dead when the heartbeat and breathing irreversibly stop, or when brain function totally and irreversibly stops, which is a condition called *brain death.* "[10] The provisions of that act permit physicians to use accepted medical standards, such as running tests to try to detect brain activity, in applying this definition.

The brain-death definition of death raises important medical, legal, and ethical questions. Supporters of this definition say that it benefits persons facing certain demise by providing vital organs for transplantation. Many medical schools have formal programs for enlisting potential organ transplant donors, and a subspecialty in hospital chaplaincy is assisting families and patients to decide whether or not to contribute organs to an organ bank linked to a national registry.

People in developed nations are being encouraged to sign an *advance directive* or *living will.* The legally signed document conveys to one's family and medical care team a person's desires about the kind of care he or she wishes to receive when near death or when unable to communicate. Furthermore, by executing a *durable power of attorney for health care* individuals appoint, in advance, a person or group to speak for them if they are unable to make medical decisions. It is more direct than a living will and can guide health care during a person's entire life span. When a person facing death has indicated he or she prefers that no heroic measures be employed to maintain life, the family is often plunged into a difficult ethical decision. Withdrawal of such treatment, sometimes including food and hydration, is called *passive euthanasia* (mercy killing). Such decisions should be made consultatively (with legal/medical/ethical advice), prayerfully, and compassionately.

A multidisciplinary approach to terminal care is practiced in modern hospitals. Ideally, the whole team of care providers—physicians, nurses, ethicists, chaplains, etc.—is equipped to respond to the broad spectrum of needs experienced in a situation of death. Your own caring experiences may have drawn you into this difficult decision-making process. Caregivers need to respond to physical, emotional, social, and spiritual issues and to do so with profound regard for the patient, family members, and one another. The tendency to act in a way that suits one's vested interests rather than the patient's true needs must be constantly challenged. An acquaintance followed her physician's advice and placed her spouse in hospice care. The man's health improved; thus, their decision was premature.

MULTICULTURAL RELIGIOUS PERSPECTIVES

Deep changes in our views of death are occurring in our increasingly interconnected world. What Christianity brings to the opinions of death and the life beyond may not be appreciated by devotees of Islam, Hinduism, Buddhism, even Judaism. Middle East analyst Abdullah Schleiffer was quoted in a *New York Times* editorial on why September 11 amounts to World War III. Schleiffer holds that 9/11 was about religious totalitarians, Islamists, using suicide bombing to try to impose the reign of the perfect faith, political Islam. Terrorism is different from previous world conflicts, noted columnist Thomas Friedman, because it disregards certain bedrock rules of civilization. "With Islamist militant groups, we face people who hate us more than they love life."[11] People ready to commit suicide as human bombs are weapons virtually impossible to detect or deter. Suicide bombers attack *trust*—the most essential element of an open society.

We are told that Sura (chapter) 36 of the Koran ends thus: "All glory to Him who controls all things! Unto Him you shall all return." The 9/11 terrorist assaults on United States targets were apparently the product of their obedience to Allah's supposed plan for the timing of their deaths. The terrorist hijackers of the ill-fated planes understood themselves as serving the will of Allah by engaging in holy war against the capitalist systems of the Western world. They willingly laid "down their lives for the things in which they believed . . . [hoping] that martyrdom would be followed by automatic entry to Paradise."[12] The horror the terrorists wrought on America and grief they caused thousands of family members of those who perished was done within the framework of religious devotion.

Our view of the hereafter impacts how we live on earth as well as how we view death. Besides Islam's "paradise," there are many other views of eternity held by various religions. The ancient Greeks believed that the souls of the dead led a shadowy existence in the underworld, called *Hades*. Hindus and Buddhists believe that the nonphysical part of a person is *reincarnated* (reborn) in different forms until, at last, the human spirit is absorbed into the ultimate divine spirit. Many African societies believe that a person's soul lives through a descendant.

An African student in a class I taught at a college near Nairobi, Kenya, reported he and his wife had twelve children—one to continue the legacy of each of their parents and grandparents. Physical immortality, they believe, lives through both patriarchal and matriarchal lines. If you have visited the Ming Tombs in China or the Egyptian pyramids of Geza, you know that great care was exercised in the burial practices to ensure that royalty went well provisioned into eternity. In such sites, archeologists have found mummified bodies, clothing, jewelry, worship objects, and weapons buried with the dead, indicating hope for an existence beyond death.

Rabbi Zalman Schachter-Shalomi, a student of world religions and founder of the Spiritual Eldering Institute in Philadelphia, relates tales of spiritual elders who died in a state of conscious readiness and acceptance.[13] He cites the dying, in 1951, of the Indian sage Sri Ramana Marharshi, whose grieving disciples begged him not to leave them. "They say I am dying," he replied, "but I am not going away. Where could I go? I am here." One eyewitness said at the end, "there was no struggle, . . . no other signs of death: only that the next breath did not come."[13]

In another reference, he reported the inspirational death of Rabbi Israel ben Eliezer, who founded the Hasidic movement in the eighteenth century. As he lay dying, Eliezer demonstrated to several close disciples how life was leaving his body, limb by limb, as his soul prepared to return to its supernal home. Just before he died, the rabbi said, "I have no worries with regard to myself. For I know . . . I am going out at one door and I shall go in at another." After his disciples prayed for Eliezer, he whispered, "My God, Lord of all worlds!" Then he quoted Psalm 36:11 (NIV): "Let not the foot of pride come upon me. With that, he peacefully expired."[14]

Such reports lead us to ask, what are some personal perspectives on this subject that is often hard for individuals to discuss? Many Americans view death as the ultimate defeat rather than as a natural part of the life cycle. This may be true, in part, because of belief in the biblical claim: "The last enemy to be destroyed is death" (1 Cor. 15:26, NIV).

PERSONAL VIEWS OF DEATH AND ETERNAL LIFE

Some people try to deal with their death anxiety by treating it as a monstrous joke—as dancing with the worms. Four decades ago, I read descriptions by Jessica Mitford of selected Americans' views of death.[15] One of the most macabre was the spoof of bodies of the deceased seen bloated (as though filled with helium), then simply floating up and away. I once heard Swiss psychiatrist Elisabeth Kübler-Ross recite the litany of "stages" of dying discovered in her University of Chicago research—from shock and denial to anger and acceptance. Her *On Death and Dying* (first published in 1969 by Macmillan) has been a standard source of wisdom about thanatology for countless caregivers. Following her death in 2004, the EKR Foundation was started to keep Elisabeth's spirit and legacy alive.

Pulitzer Prize-winning author Studs Terkel published recordings of interviews he had conducted with sixty-one representative Americans who spoke of crossing "that lonesome valley."[15] Readers learn from the stories of persons as varied as students, soldiers, an AIDS counselor, a homicide detective, a former death-row inmate, and physicians—storytellers both esteemed and unknown—about their views of death and what may come after. A Hiroshima survivor described death as saying good-bye to all attachments, including things, but most important, to bonds with people. Of the faith factor, Terkel wrote: "Invariably, those who have a faith, whether it is called religious or spiritual, have an easier time with loss. They find solace in believing there is a something after—that they will in some way, in some form, again meet or even merge with the departed one. Nonbelievers have no such comfort."[16]

Death removes people from this time/space dimension, but we try to keep them alive in our memories with pictures, treasured objects, and stories. I have been haunted by disenfranchised grief since the age of nine, when my father was killed in a tragic vehicle accident. A great heap of grief has laid buried in me since that day in May 1935 when a newspaper-delivery boy rode his bicycle up to where I was talking with friends in an elementary schoolyard and announced: "A Mr. Brister was run over in front of the Security Bank today." Although hospitalized, that critically wounded man died in less than a fortnight. Think about it! We need rituals for childhood grievers like my seven-year-old sister and myself—such as lighting a candle on the deceased person's birthday or during a family reunion—in order to focus a sense of loss and maintain continuity with the living.

Some of you may have had a near-death experience. My wife, Gloria, had a critical toxic pregnancy in 1951. By God's great mercy and the skill of two fine physicians at Baptist Hospital in New Orleans, she survived a harrowing struggle between life and death. Our son, Mark, was delivered prematurely and remained in neonatal care days after Gloria was well enough to return to our apartment. I also faced a near-death experience in my own life, Easter of 2003, following a critical angina episode.

One of the most poignant tales of the terrors of war and vivid descriptions of grim death harvests following bombings, grenade attacks, and firefights available in the English language is Tim O'Brien's novel about Vietnam combat—*The Things They Carried.*[17] However, it is his stories imbedded within accounts of smelling and seeing the corpses of war's casualties that grabbed my interest. O'Brien writes of falling in love with a lovely girl, Linda, when they were in fourth grade. Perhaps the name is a pseudonym, but "Linda" was compellingly feminine, with poise, great dignity, and a winning smile.

In September, as they entered fifth grade, Linda died with a brain tumor. Tim was catapulted into grief. He wrote of trying to imagine what it was like to be dead. In lonely moments after her burial, he whispered her name, trying to make her come back from the grave. "Linda," he begged, "please. . . ."[18] O'Brien's view of Linda's whereabouts in the afterlife was compelling reading. As a forty-three-year-old writer, he could still see her "as if through ice, as if I'm gazing into some other world, a place where there are no brain tumors, and no funeral homes, where there are no bodies at all."[19] His tale of early love is woven into the fabric of hundreds of war stories—all told, by his admission, as a way of coping with his own finitude. He admitted that he was Tim O'Brien, trying to save nine-year-old Timmy's life with a story.

The aftermath of destruction and loss of life following the massive earthquake and tsunami in southern Asia and Africa, December 2004, defied description. With some 150,000 persons reported dead, thousands more missing, and 5 million left homeless, survivors' stories were tinged with pathos. They reported walls of water unexpectedly slamming ashore—from Indonesia to Sri Lanka, from Thailand to India, even to Somalia in East Africa—at speeds up to 500 miles an hour. Humanitarian aid came quickly from many nations as the entire planet was plunged into mourning. Adherents of world religions were driven to prayer and searching their sacred scriptures for answers to such a tragedy.

BIBLICAL PERSPECTIVES ON DEATH AND THE LIFE BEYOND

"Never say die" is an audacious proposal that fails to work in real life. We may postpone death with miracle surgeries and medications—with techniques that might splice DNA and repair cell damage—but, finally, death wins its way. No where is life's end and the hereafter taken more seriously than in the Hebrew-Christian Scriptures. Cruden's Concordance lists some 260 biblical references to *death* and 525 references to *heaven*—in the sense of completion of earthly existence. Fewer than a hundred references to *Hell* appeared, with various meanings and uses—from the Hebrew Sheol, "the place of the dead" to the New Testament's use of Hades as "the place of the dead," and eight references to Gehenna as a "place of retribution for evil deeds."[20] There are many biblical metaphors picturing the life beyond, as in: *heaven,* which gives substance to the spiritual gift of hope; *eternal life,* the *redeemed,* one named in the *book of life,* the *kingdom of God*—as past, present, and future (Matt. 6:10); *the Father's house* (John 14:2, NIV); and God's *tree of life* in the garden at history's consummation (Rev. 22:2, NIV).

Following the Fall of God's first created persons through disobedience (see Gen. 3:1-14, NIV), there appears a hopeful promise of redemption in Genesis 3:15 (NIV). The Bible makes it clear that eternal life was *not* granted to humankind at creation, but God did pledge an ultimate victory over evil and death. The New Testament recounts the advent of God's son, Jesus the Christ, and, through his saving life, death, and resurrection, the promise of eternal life so "we may live together with him" (1 Thess. 5:10, NIV).

In the following section, I draw heavily on the work of Jurgen Moltmann, author of *In the End—the Beginning: The Life of Hope.*[21] Moltmann, one of the foremost religious thinkers in the world, is Professor Emeritus of Theology at the University of Tubingen, Germany. Moltmann holds that Christianity issued from a catastrophe, the dark horror of the passion on Golgotha of the Messiah Jesus by the Roman-occupying forces in Jerusalem. Jesus the Christ came preaching that "the kingdom of God is at hand: repent," not in the Old Covenant sense of judgment, but in grace (Mark 1:15, NIV). In Christ, God came to meet human beings and to redeem them from sin, evil, and injustice through the Cross.

Christ's redeeming death was not the end, but the beginning of life anew through his resurrection from the dead. He became "the first fruits of those who have fallen asleep," as the Apostle Paul wrote; for "in Christ all will be made alive" (1 Cor. 15:20-22, NIV). Christ's postresurrection appearances both astonished his followers and persuaded them to believe in the reality of life after death (see Rom. 1:1-6, NIV). It was not merely his spirit that appeared to them, it was Jesus himself in the transfigured form of the resurrection world, noted Moltmann. Consequently, Christ's resurrection is more than a past event; it guarantees future life, beyond the grave, for true believers. Caregivers of varied religious persuasions recognize that, in theological language, the resurrection is an *eschatological* event. God's future has already begun and ensures victory over death for all time.

Bonded irrevocably to Christ's resurrection event is God's pledge of eternal life to all persons who believe (i.e., commit their lives) in Jesus Christ. True believers have "died to sin. All of us who were baptized into Christ Jesus were baptized into his death. We were therefore buried with him through baptism into death in order that, just as Christ was raised from the dead . . . we too may live a new life" (Romans 6:1-4, NIV).

Images of heaven appear in Revelation 21 and 22—more than a state—a place filled with God's glory; no night there but celestial light; a place of continual worship, where there will be "no more death . . . or crying . . . or pain." Jesus said that all persons who hear and heed the gospel message are ensured eternal life—here and now, as well as in heaven (see John 3:1-17, NIV). But the opposite is also true! Alongside God's righteousness is his eternal justice. Jesus warned: "Whoever does *not* believe stands condemned already because he has not believed in the name of God's one and only Son" (John 3:18ff, NIV). Unbelief, sinning against the light, is viewed as the path to spiritual death.

In biblical imagery, God is "himself the eternal home of everything he has created. . . . In the end God gathers everything into himself."[22] The Christian hope resides in the promise, envisioned now "through a glass darkly," that God's children are homeward bound (1 Cor. 13:12, NIV). At last, everything God has created will dwell in God and remain true to its unique character. It is in this hope, wrote Paul, "that we are saved" (Rom 8:18-24a, NIV). Moltmann observed further that just as everything is in God, so God is present in all things and interpenetrates their finitude with his infinity.[23] The biblical picture of God's kingdom in his glory is that "God [will] be all in all" (1 Cor. 15:28b, NIV). To be with God in his glory, as the hymn writer wrote, "will be glory for me."

CONCLUDING THOUGHT

Before we conclude, someone may ask, "Is there a word for the living to brace us for life's traumas and disappointments, for the surprises and risks of human existence?" Yes, I have found what Katherine Fischer calls "winter grace" by learning to harvest dividends from investments made in other persons—enjoying family—mentoring younger sojourners, and by remembering the privileges and contributions of a lifetime. Jewish rabbi Zalman Schachter-Shalomi described harvest time thus: "We reach the summit in life in the October, November, and December of our lives as we enjoy the fruits of the harvest and replant the seed for the next crop."[24] He reminds retirees that earthly life is more than a vestibule to eternity. We can enjoy the fruits of a lifetime "on this side" rather than only in the world to come.

Theologian-counselor Kathleen Fischer emphasizes both the personal and social dimensions of Christian hope in her *Winter Grace: Spirituality and Aging*. In discussing *resurrection*, Fischer notes

> since resurrection faith means that what happened to Jesus will also happen to us . . . this includes a communion with all persons

which is deeper and more extensive than we have known. . . . The New Testament makes clear that resurrection is a community experience.[25]

What if you are unsure of what to say or how to converse with a terminally ill person? In the Appendix for Caregivers, provided at this book's conclusion, you will find suggestions on the art of supportive conversation. Meanwhile, we all need guidance in seeking to find our way *home*.

A SUMMARY OF KEY POINTS

- Because death is a universal human experience, philosophers and writers through the ages have provided reflections on this compelling, mysterious, topic. One of the key contributions of a biblical worldview is the assurance of true believers' eternal life with God rather than mere theories or speculations about immortality.
- Biologically, human beings are terminal. The body, while "fearfully and wonderfully made," is like a fine machine that must be kept in good repair. Because of advances in medical technology, many steps are now being taken to prolong, not merely improve, life.
- Across the centuries, all major world religions have constructed theologies of death, dying, and the life beyond. We noted that Christianity's views of death and resurrection, disclosed in the Scriptures, are distinct from other conceptions held by devotees of Islam, Hinduism, Buddhism, even Judaism.
- Personal testimonies from the author and others were viewed against the concluding backdrop of biblical perspectives on death, resurrection, and eternal life. Ultimately, true believers will be welcomed to their heavenly home by the creator God.

Chapter 9

Finding Your Way Home

The yearning for a lasting *home* is a universal human condition. Through the ages, persons have asked wistfully: "Is this all there is to life or is there something more?" Whatever your national origin, present age, gender, clan, or native language, you may have wondered what existence is like beyond this life. *Home,* as I am using the term, embraces what some persons call "the eternity factor in daily life." Like Steven Spielberg's "E. T.—The Extra-Terrestrial," when human beings look through the prism of time, they are searching for an ultimate habitation.

The ancient writer of Ecclesiastes observed that the Creator "set eternity in the hearts of [everyone]; yet, they cannot fathom what God has done from beginning to end" (Eccles. 3:11, NIV). What does *eternity* mean in such a poetic context? The author struggled with the question: "How can life best be lived?" Likely, the sage inferred that God placed the desire to understand the past and future in human hearts but has withheld crucially important knowledge that you and I desire.

The late Christopher Reeve's tragic horse-riding mishap and courage in facing lifelong paralysis is a metaphor for all persons who wonder about being and time, evil and suffering, life and death—in reality, about finding the way to one's ultimate abode. Reeve's brave heart that carried him to unexplored realms of hope fell silent October 10, 2004, at the age of fifty-two. A sign hung in the late Superman's exercise room: "For everyone who thought I couldn't do it. . . . For everyone who said, 'It's impossible.' See you at the finish line."[1] Reeve's "finish line," however, was not the *final* line—simply a pause between eternities. His physical death was the penultimate, not the

Spiritual Wisdom for Successful Retirement
Published by The Haworth Press, Inc. 2006. All rights reserved.
doi:10.1300/5537_10

ultimate, finish. Although I appreciated his spiritual qualities, such as: courage, love of family, inspiring example, unbounded optimism, and desire for a cure for his paralysis, I failed to see any reference to his religious orientation or affiliation with a community of faith.

World religions make explicit how humankind's spiritual longings have become codified into formalized expression. Spirituality is personal, whereas religion is institutional. Different expressions of religious faith tell us how to believe and behave on earth. Religions also point us to a future story—to resurrection and an afterlife, eternal bliss, nirvana, purgatory, to reincarnation, soul sleep, or, for the condemned, to eternal damnation. Ministers, priests, sages, and prophets—men and women of high callings and sacred vows—are principal characters of religious rituals and devotion, history, legend, and folk myths.

Superman Reeve's world of fame and fortune disappeared in an accident. Change constantly sweeps away our security with uncertainties, such as the giant tsunami waves in South Asia in December 2004. Millions of people were rendered homeless in a matter of seconds. Finding your way *home,* as we shall consider it here, is coming to terms with the Ultimate, a mid life's immediacies.[2] In a biblical worldview, a person is *at home* who accepts by faith the gift of God's acceptance and lives with certitude about his or her eternal destiny (Rom. 14:8-9, NIV). Without an authentic faith in an afterlife there is no recognition of losing or finding one's eternal home—one's true self—hidden in God.

One of the clearest biblical pictures of home loss and the significance of its recovery is presented in the story of the Prodigal Son (Luke 15:11-32, NIV). The waiting father in the story symbolizes the forgiving Redeemer God. Hear his words to the unforgiving elder brother: "We had to celebrate and be glad, because this brother of yours was dead and is alive again; he was lost and is found" (Luke 15:32, NIV). The lost son came to his senses when he recognized his place was in his father's house—a foregleam of true believers' glad reunion with God and the redeemed.

With my use of *home* clarified, let us explore the universal quest for a lasting home. What we learn together may help you forge a future with hope.

THE LONGING TO BELONG

Home, like time, is not easy to define. Webster tells us the word *home* comes from the Old English *ham* = *village;* akin to the Greek *koiman* = "to be still, calm, quiet," literally "to put to sleep." Home is our birthing place—whether a tribal village or a vast metropolis—so that we are anchored in the relationships, land, language, lore, lessons, rituals, stories, smells, and memories of a location. Our abode is also our residing place of choice, chance, or circumstance. Ultimately, our homeland is where we elect to build a house of faith and hope to reside for eternity.

Our longing to belong is exemplified in the transitory feelings of the African writer, M. G. Vassanji, who started life in an Indian neighborhood of Nairobi, Kenya. When he was five, his father died of a heart attack and his mother moved the family to Dar es Salaam, Tanzania. Today, Vasssanji lives in Toronto, but he has lived literally all over the world. His nomadic existence has not always been of his choosing. At the age of nineteen, Vassanji left the University of Nairobi, having received a scholarship to Massachusetts Institute of Technology, where he studied nuclear physics, and later earned a PhD at the University of Pennsylvania. He worked for a time at a nuclear power plant in Ontario before moving to Toronto in 1980 and taking up writing as a career. His prize-winning novels, including *The Gunny Sack* and *The Book of Secrets,* closely follow modern African history and politics.

While living in a transitory world much of his life, Vassanji reflected a deep longing to belong. He clearly champions Africa, although he has become a Canadian citizen. He wrote of the past, "Anyone who's gone through it certainly knows the disappointment and the betrayal in the whole of Africa. . . . Basically we became pawns of the Old World powers."[3] In many respects, the permanence of place eluded Vassanji as he was swept along in family problems, political upheavals, migrations, and deaths. There is sadness in his lament: "I feel a sense of belonging that's never fulfilled." His homecoming remains an unrealized potential.

Experiences of separation from one's place and people, such as Vassanji's, are almost universal for retired persons. A seventy-two-year-old retiree, Jim, described his nomadic existence as a youth in school, in a bounce-around-the-world military career, in and out of various jobs, and, finally, as a human resources manager in a major steel plant. With foreign steel products, often of inferior grades and cheaper prices than U.S. steel flooding world markets, his steel mill closed. Jim did not leave the community he loved, but his vocation left him. Fortunately, his willingness to volunteer stood him in good stead. His Christian congregation became his earthly family. Today, this retired senior is a key leader in his religious community.

It is not easy to exit the demanding world of work and cycle down to the slower pace of retirement living. A friend of mine described his feelings of being at "loose ends" and searching for a place at the close of his paid employment:

> I seem to have turned seventy-four this week and am still trying to figure out what it means to be retired. My theory is that I should do some of the old stuff . . . as long as I can and try to balance that with something new that keeps my anxiety in working order. So I am still doing some of the old. I do some individual consultation with pastors and some couples therapy. . . . As to the new, which is also old (I quit this for thirty-five years) I'm taking jazz piano and saxophone lessons and playing in two bands. The jazz theory stuff really pushes me, but by the time I'm eighty I fantasize that I'll be one ___ of a player. In between times I try to keep up with 10 grandchildren (all 10 years and younger . . .). Thank God for Helen for that and many other reasons.[4]

The longing to belong runs like a scarlet thread through this vignette of a retired man's fantasies. He is out of work but still at work. He quit music lessons and playing instruments some thirty-five years ago but is back at the jazz game again. He has long since gone out of the parenting business but now seeks to shepherd ten grandchildren, along with the help of his wife. John is also a writer in the pastoral care field and has promise of another book release soon.

The wandering Indian writer Vassanji, now legally residing in Toronto; the former steel mill executive whose vocational home left him; and my friend—each of these adults seeks a permanent place and people. I call such searching the longing for inner home. In some respects unattached retirees are like the sky dancers I saw recently on television, suspended by cables from above the stage. They were there, but not here—anchored securely by gravity to earth. The sky dancers dangled, twisting and turning in artistic motion, belonging neither to land nor to sky. That free-floating feeling may characterize your own experience, because many retirees resist the impermanence that rules the physical world.

THE LAND BETWEEN

To retire implies "to take out of use." However, most retirees prefer to maintain relationships and continue usefulness. Our high-tech society, enamoured with constant innovation, makes retired persons feel redundant and obsolete. Os Guinness, Senior Fellow of the Trinity Forum in Washington, DC, affirms in his book, *The Call,* that we never retire from our calling. No longer on the job, yet hearing the Caller's voice, many retired persons occupy *the land between.*

While visiting Hong Kong, I noted an idyllic description of the New Territories, the vast land linking Hong Kong's 230 islands and the Kowloon Peninsula with the China mainland. "The land between" separates the hectic pace of life in Hong Kong from the tranquil mountains, forests, fishing villages, and farms to the north. This physical boundary is a metaphor for our present existence in time/space while awaiting the future dimension of endless time.

John Weir Perry wrote: "When we look at the world under the aspect of eternity, life is animated in ways that constantly astound us."[5] In every world culture, it is the retirees and the elderly who remain most aware of "the land between." Here, I use *land between* as our consciousness, while living here and now, of an abode outside the finite limits of earth. Beyond our childhood beginnings and current living arrangements lies a future place cloaked in our hopes, dreams, and sacred imaginations. It is our habitation of ultimate desire and faith commitment, described in the Book of Revelation as a place of glad reunions, of endless time, of security, where there is no terror, pain, disease, sin, or death. The Bible calls that place *heaven*—a place of belonging, joyful worship, meaningful service, tranquil fulfillment, and blessed relationships.

Retirees are offered many options to bridge the time/space gap between leaving an occupation and experiencing their mortality. They pursue activities of unfinished lives—from limited employment to leisure travel, from meaningful volunteerism to playing golf or tennis, from visiting family and friends to medical consultations, and from endless worrying to hobbies, reading, or advanced study. Some retirees appear unable to get themselves off their hands. Many seniors are constrained by physical limitations but prefer not to be a "bother." So, they pray and piddle, gossip and garden, travel and take medication, fantasize future stories and face gathering gloom, keep a full date book, and, occasionally, feel worthless. Single seniors enjoy companions yet experience inner loneliness. Emotionally healthy retirees seek to face life with courage not despair.

Power slips from the grasp of residents of the land between. Men and women of enormous talent, physical endurance, fame, fortune, patriotism, loyalty, and devotion may "fall through the cracks" of a youth-oriented culture. Fathers who have generated family-owned businesses may seek to splice adult children into the company management structure—with great success or to no avail. It all depends on a thousand variables—from intergenerational talent to temperament, from strength of imagination to weakness of will, from jealousy to trust, and from high control needs to freedom. Retirees' reactions to their new, powerless status differ—from honest recognition ("I no longer have a portfolio, a title, a schedule"), to whimpering complaints, to courageous optimism.

You will be inspired by the remarkable story of a survivor who makes his home in the land between. Dr. Jules Lodish, a hematologist and oncologist, has lived ten years with amyotrophic lateral sclerosis (ALS), a progressive, paralyzing disease. Paralyzed, with nearly every muscle stilled, he communicates with the help of a computer speaker by typing with twitches of his cheek, detected by a sensor clipped to his glasses. When asked how he feels about life, Lodish responds: "I still look forward to every day."[6]

ALS, or Lou Gehrig's disease, has sometimes been described as a living death in which the body goes flaccid while the mind remains intact and acutely aware. With adequate medical care, patients may live relatively free of physical pain from the disease itself. "It's more a sort of existential, psychic sort of pain," noted Dr. Leo McCluskey, a Philadelphia neurologist who treats patients with the disease. As a result, patients and their families are forced, on a daily basis, to take stock of the meaning and quality of their lives and to make hard choices about how much is too much.

Reporters of the Lodish case note that "what keeps many patients alive . . . is a sense of having unfinished business—perhaps a milestone like getting the last kid off to college." They quote Dr. Linda Ganzini, a psychiatry professor at Oregon Health and Science University in Portland, who has studied patients making end-of-life decisions: "With ALS, you have a choice about when to stop treatment" and let nature take its course.[7] Many patients, Ganzini noted, have deep religious beliefs that help sustain them, and they are able "to find hope in the future, find meaning and tolerate the daily ongoing losses that they are experiencing."

In patient Lodish's case, he has devised a thirty-page guide for his nurses that sets standards for a sterile environment that go beyond hospital practices. His rules have helped him avoid the infections that kill many patients. He survives on a liquid nutrient recipe that he devised—including ingredients that are kosher—that flow down his feeding tube. My hunch is that survivor, such as Dr. Lodish, have discovered "true North" in their developing years and, now, draw dividends from lifelong investments in hope.

TRUE NORTH

To finish life well you must select your destination with care, choose your companions wisely, chart your course, and follow trusted points on the compass. Peter F. Drucker, now deceased, described this process as repositioning oneself for effectiveness and enjoyment in the second half of life. For ages, trekkers have used the stars for guidance—across the desert, over the seas, and through the air. On clear nights in northern climes, a navigator scans the skies for the North Star and uses it as a guiding beacon toward his destination. Yet, as Montaigne cautioned, "No wind favors him who has no destined port."

Retired persons, similarly, are trekkers and mapmakers in their own right. Often, they rely on the reported experiences of retirement pioneers who might point the way. Are there reliable signposts leading from the land between retirement and one's final destination? Let us consider some selected signs—characteristics, qualities, or practices—along the journey that may help you find the way home. First is the attitude of hopefulness or expectancy.

Living with Hopeful Expectancy

The pull of the past exerts a powerful force on all the anticipated actions of retired persons. I was intrigued by a man's recounting the history of his family's generations from early American beginnings to their tombstone markers in cemeteries in the deep South. His ancestors had struggled with family crises, financial concerns, attacks from Indian tribes, fears about health, tales of their fathers' exploits, to questions about the future. We can certainly learn from our forebears' achievements and contributions, as well as their shortcomings and limitations, but do we have to lock ourselves into the past?

In contrast, upon his reelection for a second term as president of the United States, George W. Bush encouraged his supporters with these words: "Because we have done the hard work, we are entering a season of hope." Living with hopeful expectancy, with positive faith in divine providence, must avoid presumption. Hopefulness embraces one's willingness to write a future story, no matter the season of one's life—youth, adulthood, or elderhood. However, true hope that wards against dissolution and destructiveness must be tempered by experience, humility, and accrued wisdom. Regarding the outcome of a U.S. presidential race, former presidential adviser David R. Gergen cautioned about falling into the trap of hubris. "When presidents win their first elections they and their teams think they are kings of the hill; when they win re-election, they too often think they are masters of the universe."[8] Presumption can often lead to mistakes of excessive pride.

Sojourners who work alongside people who may be tainted with pessimism know of "the hopeless case"—someone who has given in to fate or despair. Current events sometimes plunge people into depression. You may have read of homicides or suicides as instant responses to a broken engagement, loss of a position, a cancer diagnosis, or failure in school. Fortunately, we can help inquirers look at life with a wide-angle lens and see a larger, longer picture. We can help hope-seekers recall how the centuries speak to the hours. Biblical history, for example, relates how the Jews, who were people of faith and hope, despite tribulation, clung to the expectation that the Messiah would come and the world would get better.

Many years ago, I visited with the famed Kansas psychiatrist Karl Menninger, who, later, gave me an inscribed a copy of his autobiographical reflections, *Sparks*. There, he repeated his thesis in *Love Against Hate* that "hope [is] the dim awareness of unconscious wishes which, like dreams, tend to come true."[9] Dr. Karl was a practicing Presbyterian layman who, reportedly, taught a Bible class for many of his adult years of medical practice in Topeka. He rightly anchored his views of hope in the Scriptures, often citing the Apostle Paul's "these things remain" poem in 1 Corinthians 13 (NIV). "Hope is humble, it is modest, it is self-less," said Menninger. "Unconcerned with the ambiguity of past experience, hope implies process; it is an adventure, a going forward, a confident search." The wise physician knew that hope must be distinguished from optimism, wishful thinking or shallow expectancy—traits that are often self-centered.

Practice Gratitude and Garner Goodwill

Hans Selye, late Director of the Institute of Experimental Medicine and Surgery at the University of Montreal, was one of the world's foremost researchers on the subject of *stress*. His early medical studies, published as *The Stress of Life* by McGraw-Hill in 1956, expressed some informal afterthoughts on the importance of gratitude in stress management. Later, he confessed that, at that time, he failed to attach much importance to such psychological considerations because he was preoccupied with biochemical mechanisms governing diseases of stress and adaptation.

He was surprised by the interest expressed among psychologists, sociologists, anthropologists, and clergymen of different faiths on the emotion of gratitude's influence on physical health. He was asked to elaborate his findings, contrasting the costly effects of revenge with the healing effects of gratitude in churches, synagogues, and at conventions of diverse professional groups. Nearly two decades later, he wrote: "I came to realize that 'gratitude' is only one aspect of the broader concept of love, which has been used historically to encompass all positive feelings toward others, including respect, goodwill, sympathy, and most forms of approval and admiration."[10] Selye advocated selfish altruism—caring for others as a means of self-preservation. In human terms, noted Selye, altruistic egotism means deliberately helping others in order to gain their goodwill and trust for *your* good. This hoard of goodwill gives you a sense of security and self-esteem to cushion you against life's unavoidable hurts and frustrations. Selye's motto: *Earn* your neighbor's love.

As mentioned in an earlier chapter, an inspiring example of gratitude expressed and lived out is that of the late D. Elton Trueblood. Before his death, the Earlham philosopher published fifteen essays of appreciation for individuals who had influenced or contributed something unique to his life. These were followed by seven essays about places where he had visited or lived—from Iona, Scotland, to Shakertown, Kentucky—that he and Mrs. Trueblood appreciated. Then, he enumerated eleven educational settings—from Haverford College to Stanford University—where he had studied, lectured, or taught across the years.

Trueblood introduced his essays by reflecting on the autumn season's quiet loveliness in relationship to the life course. He called autumn of the year "a parable of human life" in which the slower pace of life is itself a remarkable blessing. The philosopher quoted a conversation from Plato's *Republic* that occurred between Socrates and Cephalus, in which Socrates is reported as saying,

> There is nothing which for my part I like better, Cephalus, than conversing with aged men; for I regard them as travelers who have gone on a journey which I too may have to go, and of whom I ought to inquire whether the way is smooth and easy, or rugged and difficult. . . . Is life harder toward the end?

The essence of the old man's reply was that "old age has a great sense of calm and freedom."[11] Having heard Trueblood speak on several occasions, I could tell that he was living out his credo of nurturing the practice of gratitude for all that is right in life. Furthermore, he seemed thankful that things are no worse than they are.

My wife and I have recently returned from an extensive lecture tour in Hong Kong and Taiwan. We were guests of several of my former doctoral students who now work, teach, and serve in Asian countries. Professor Desmond Chi Keung Choi and his student Ms. Chen Sau-wai had completed the Chinese translation of my HarperSan Francisco book *Pastoral Care in the Church* (third edition revised) and had worked with the publisher to ensure its availability when we arrived in Taipei. A team of my doctoral students accompanied Mrs. Brister and me to the publisher's offices where we were received with a tea and an autograph party.

Later, I explained to a colleague my deep appreciation for enjoying that harvest-time experience of life.

> I have sown the seeds of pastoral care, counseling, and congregational leadership principles for forty-five years. What a joy to see those seed, now a full harvest, producing a new crop of church leaders and care providers in another part of the world!

Having reached the fourscore mark, I confess that Asian experience was an exercise in humility. Being in other lands, immersed in "foreign" languages, and depending on guides who knew their way around and through some of Asia's great cities were humbling experiences.

Cultivate Generosity

Acquiring new attitudes and habits is a challenge for older retired persons, but revisioning and new perspectives are transforming experiences. You may have discovered, along with millions of other seniors, that you have accumulated a lot of "stuff" through the years. You may have saved too much—from notes in college chemistry to university yearbooks, from luggage collected over forty or more years to clothing you've been replacing for decades, and from unused garden tools to dated correspondence. Acquisitions, like our memories, are more enjoyable when they are put in some order. One of the best solutions for the overabundance of possessions is to eliminate things that are no longer useful or of value at this stage of life. Give some (even cherished) things away to save your heirs the trouble.

You may recall Jesus' story of what traditionally has been named "the parable of the rich fool" (Luke 12:13-21, NIV). You see the grasp of greed in the face of the rich man who tore down his barns and built larger ones in order to store his harvest. He then said to himself, "'You have plenty of good things laid up for many years. Take life easy; eat, drink and be merry.' But God said to him, 'You fool! This very night your life will be demanded from you.'" The seriousness of his sin is recognized when we note the textual word for "life" is not *bios,* physical life, but *psyche,* his totality as a person, his true self.

Pastoral theologian Edward Thornton sees in this account not merely greed but the evil of fear as the opposite of love. He wrote:

> A decision to seek security in material things automatically withers the soul. Fear dictates a decision to make yourself rich. In yielding to fear, you lose the opportunity to make your [true] *self* rich—to discover the joy of being centered in your true self, or being at one with God.[12]

A generous heart tunes itself, ideally, to the very character of God, demonstrated in the humility of Christ's incarnation (see Phil. 2:1-11, NIV).

Has the time come in your experience for conscious distribution rather than of accumulation? Perhaps you do not have to save everything for old age, for you are rapidly getting there. When I called a friend recently to wish him a pleasant birthday, he acknowledged chuckling (without giving his exact age): "In fifteen more years, I'll be 100!" Gaining freedom from *getting,* from desiring to acquire more things, can free you for acts of generosity toward those nearest you, toward friends and acquaintances, extended to strangers, even your enemies. Generosity includes more than money. It expresses its giving spirit in acts of friendliness, kindness, compassion, and willingness to listen to and pray for others.

Psychiatrist Harold G. Koenig has provided caregivers, indeed all persons who would demonstrate the spirit of giving, a splendid guide in his *Purpose and Power in Retirement: New Opportunities for Meaning and Significance.* He concludes his classic essay on gaining purpose and power through generosity by challenging readers to transcend a self-absorbed life. To quote his wisdom:

> Often it is not until later in life that a person cries out in existential despair: "Is there any more to life than this?" The answer is yes—there is more, but it's only accessible by cultivating a spirit of generosity.[13]

This spirit issues in surrender to God and seeks to bless others. Giving moves the generous person toward the nature of God's own self.

Something of that transformation occurs over and over in human experience as one seeks to move, in executive Bob Buford's words, toward *Finishing Well.*[14] It is said that toward the end of his life Albert Einstein moved two portraits from his office wall and replaced them with two others. He removed the portraits of two scientists whose research had led to major discoveries—Sir Isaac Newton and famed Scottish physicist James Clerk Maxwell. In their places he hung the portraits of Hindu religious leader and social reformer Mohandas K. Gandhi and the Christian missionary physician in Africa, Albert Schweitzer. His heroes had become self-giving icons, each of whom had finished life well.

To summarize, earth's sojourners are restless until they make peace with their Creator. I have called this process "finding one's inner home"—one's authentic, core self anchored in God. Finding your way home may offer some surprises, diversions, satisfactions, and detours, such as accidents, illnesses, failed business ventures, and betrayals by family members or trusted friends. For earth's teachable trekkers the course toward home becomes clearer, like a path of dawning light, as one matures. The search for home is old and, being old, it is eternal. Life's quest is motivated by the longing to belong to Someone and to join hands with "the others" in authentic community. Like Pilgrim in John Bunyan's *The Pilgrim's Progress,* seekers inevitably spend time on the uneven roadways of "the land between." They do not arrive automatically or magically at the Celestial City's gates.

Retirees must have realistic objectives in mind as they chart life's path. Your determination to reach your ultimate destination must be clear and unswerving—even in the face of evil and death. To find your way home, from the land between to eternity, you must select your destination, chart your course, and follow trusted points on the compass with great care. When you arrive home at last, you will discover that you are what you have been all along, in your essence, only more so. Because our Creator is infinite love and our Maker's dwelling place is your goal, hopefully you are already bonded in a transforming relationship with God who is your all in all.

A SUMMARY OF KEY POINTS

- We first noted that *home* is used in this chapter to infer "the eternity factor in daily life"; furthermore, certain persons in all cultures, at all times, experienced the eternity factor in their hearts (Eccles. 3:11, NIV).

- *Home,* in this usage, includes "the longing to belong," navigating "the land between," and charting one's life course with aid of the spiritual "North Star."
- Three major guideposts were noted to arrive at the Celestial City of eternity: living with hopeful expectancy, practicing gratitude, and being unselfishly generous.

Chapter 10

Keeping Life in Balance

"I'm hanging it up," my colleague of many years said as he strolled along a familiar hall corridor of the main campus building. A native of Illinois, he had moved to Texas in the 1940s, completed a doctorate in biblical studies, then joined the theological school faculty as Instructor of Hebrew and Old Testament. Jim and his wife, Aletha, eventually moved from a "starter" house into a classic two-story home near the Texas Christian University campus. In addition to raising four children, all with notable careers themselves, he taught thousands of future ministers and missionaries and published major books in his chosen field.

Jim's droll humor, high-pitched lecturing voice, brilliant mind, and winsome spirit won him acclaim from colleagues and scholars in professional guilds. A respected churchman and Bible class teacher, he was truly a man without guile. My wife, son, and I cared for Hoshek (which means "black" in Hebrew), the Smiths' pet dog, during Jim's sabbatical leave year at Harvard University. Gloria and I visited the retired couple regularly, usually with small gifts of baked goods or fruit. The camaraderie we shared was a gift of a lifetime. Something of his spirit remains with us to this day.

But Jim was more than a husband, father, scholar, author, churchman, and later, father-in-law, grandfather, and friend. He enjoyed baseball, was an avid golfer, and practiced his swing as long as he could walk the fairways of local golf courses. (Yes, he preferred to pull a golf cart around eighteen holes—for fellowship and exercise—rather than ride in an electric cart.) More important, he was a man of faith, anchored to God, and constant in prayer. Tall and lean, he had learned to care for his body as a temple of the Spirit. He modeled a life of healthy balance. Friends noticed that when Jim retired, he *left*

Spiritual Wisdom for Successful Retirement
Published by The Haworth Press, Inc. 2006. All rights reserved.
doi:10.1300/5537_11

the workplace and began a whole new life. He learned to use a computer and taught himself Spanish in retirement.

RETIREMENT CHANGES (ALMOST) EVERYTHING

We are told that, on average, 5,000 Americans retire each day, although many of them have not reached the traditional retirement age of sixty-five. Retirees come in both genders, spanning stages from youthful zest to elderly reserve, and from all walks of life. A study by the U.S. Administration on Aging projects that by the year 2030 there will be more than seventy million Americans over age sixty-five. The majority of them will experience traditional retirement at some point in their lives.

You read in the book's Introduction that, as we age, life tumbles in upon us with a thousand serendipities—gifts, crises, hopes, fears, limitations, joys, and possibilities. We have to let go of some things whether we want to or not. Retired persons struggle with real and symbolic losses—attempting to keep life in balance—while facing uncertain futures, broken dreams, altered living arrangements, and physical limitations. The future seldom unfolds precisely the way we plan. Disappointments, adversity, and suffering open us to the spiritual domain. What we do know is that we will have a choice of responses—from paralyzing fear to hope.

Profound identity and status changes prompted by retirement evoke varied responses from retirees. When two lifestyles—from paid employment to nonpaid redundancy—encounter each other for the first time, they differ in their respective degree of diversity, complexity, and potency. Letting go of who we were—whether a machinist, rancher, pilot, clerk, teacher, chef, soldier, or physician—prompts a real sense of loss. Thus, feelings of grief mixed with a sense of relief overshadow the loss of "the way we were."

This fact was visibly demonstrated during the Olympic Games in Athens, Greece, in August 2004, when American wrestler Rulon Gardner fought his last match. In the 2000 Sydney games, the Afton, Wyoming, native had stunned the sports world by beating the Russian superstar Alexander Karelin in the wrestling upset of the century. With memories of that gold medal still fresh, Gardner was forced to settle for a bronze in Athens because of an overtime loss to Georgi Tsurtsumia of Kazakhstan. In the traditional sign of retirement in wrestling, Gardner sat on the mat, an American flag draped in his arms, removed his shoes, and placed them in the center of the ring. Tears were streaming down his face.[1]

Gardner's grief became evident even before the match, when he told coach Steve Fraser that he planned to retire. "That's it," Gardner said. "When you step off the mat for the last time, it's a big deal." A sportswriter noted that placing his shoes in the ring ended a remarkable career that saw Gardner become one of America's most improbable sports stars—and one of its most star-crossed once he had won the gold. Now, the 264-pound Olympian can slow down, explore new pathways of interest, and come to terms with a new identity.

When you "put your shoes into the retirement ring"—whether by choice or circumstances—change happens. As a geologist expressed it, "When I retired every day became Saturday" (i.e., a free from paid employment day). His business card read, in addition to his name: "Retired. Gone fishing." His humorous self-identification conveyed a serious message. There was no longer a daily ritual of rising and leaving for work that gave meaning and structure to his life. Fortunately, along with exploring for oil and investing in land, Joe was a rancher and had chores to look forward to. Not every retiree is so fortunate. Their days are filled with "Honey dos," trips to physicians' offices, fretting about bills, watching TV, considering reemployment options, and managing time on their hands.

Rather than being victimized by the open-endedness of such new freedom, or by the need to rush into volunteerism or to get a part-time job, retirees need *the humility just to be*. As the respected rabbi Abraham Joshua Heschel noted: "Just to be is a blessing, just to live is holy."[2] Recognition of the Holy involves reframing your point of view—sensing that you matter to God and to other persons—and that life will go on. Responsible retirement involves both deeply held personal core values and community (social) accountability. For retirement to be both enjoyed and embraced, you must have a responsible purpose for doing life—for pursuing new goals.

Such a spiritual stance requires what ethicist Rushworth Kidder describes as a "morality of mindfulness."[3] Kidder worked as a senior columnist for the *Christian Science Monitor* before founding The Institute for Global Ethics in Camden, Maine. In his attempt to resolve the dilemmas of ethical living in an age of distraction and disruption, Kidder advocates intentional decision making. He rightly observes that so many of life's dilemmas involve moral decisions, not between right and wrong but between right versus right as responsible persons try to pursue worthy goals.

Retirees seeking to build some structure into their lives, based on spiritual convictions, may find Kidder's four ethical dilemma paradoxes useful. He introduces a *right versus right* notion at the book's outset and then elaborates as the discussion unfolds. Our decisions revolve around four options, he notes: deciding between truth versus loyalty, between individual and community priorities, between short term and long-term outcomes of decisions, and between justice and mercy.

In concluding his typological explanations, Kidder committed himself as follows:[4]

- Regarding Truth versus Loyalty choices, he cites examples of leaders who required loyalty, such as Hitler, Mao, Stalin, and Saddam Hussein. Then he says: "I feel safer and more comfortable honoring what is true than following human allegiances."
- Regarding Individual versus Community values, he writes: "Compelled to chose between individual and community *good,* I would lean toward the community." He suggests ordering life for the common good rather than for personal rights and privileges. Such goals must remain flexible because retirees often experience health concerns and other restrictions that may require modification of pursuits.
- In choosing between Short- and Long-Term outcomes of decisions, Kidder favors long-term effects because they generally include short-term outcomes.
- Kidder prefers Mercy over Justice, he says, because mercy speaks of love and compassion. Ethicists like Paul Tillich and Reinhold Niebuhr would go further and say that humankind has yet to explore fully the justice that may be found in *agape* love. Although these options cannot make choices for us, they can help us with the sticky wickets of ambiguous decisions. Let us keep this model in mind as we consider ways to keep life in balance.

The retiree's new calling involves choices among all the opportunities, options, distractions, calls for help, and disappointments life may bring. A life of balanced priorities gathers all the strands of existence and weaves the threads into a single garment of spiritual strength, service, and satisfaction.

MANAGING PRIORITIES

Counselors Richard and Linda Eyre claim that healthy *balance* is a prevailing personal challenge in the Western world.[5] In their guidebook, *Lifebalance,* they contend that survival was the challenge before the industrial revolution. Thereafter, the big challenge was physical and economic quality of life. Now, they say, it is difficult to balance our time. It is demanding to balance our thought and our attention. It is tough to balance our resources and our desires. "And because we have so many options, alternatives, choices, and opportunities, it's hard to balance our priorities."[6] Destructive stress typifies lives of driven persons who are always striving upward for the next level of "whatever."

Retired persons are not immune from the struggle between former life patterns and changing new demands. True, we no longer have the demands of work and the pressure of career, but many retirees are still family persons whose children and grandchildren require attention and assistance. Our extended family members expect our involvement in their lives. Friends desire our company for shopping, attending worship, travel, and recreational activities such as bridge, bowling, and golf. Fitness programs, along with talking by phone and communicating by e-mail, consume retirees' hours.

Personal interests demand recognition and fulfillment—from volunteer ministries, to leisure activities, to self-care, including long waits in the offices of health care professionals. Skills we could not pursue when we were younger, interests we could not develop at earlier stages of life, talents we could not employ when work took priority in our lives—all these clamor for attention. Community organizations and religious activities want portions of our time and energy. During retirement years, people find it difficult to balance the needs, demands, and interests of life.

Sociological and psychological assumptions that inform retirement theory tend to overlook the spiritual dimensions of human consciousness. Persons of religious persuasion realize that life's priorities have an eternal as well as a temporal reality. Exploring any human issue to its ultimate depth leads to a spiritual baseline. By *spiritual*, I imply considerations of human existence connected with God—the reality of the Holy—and with the Creator's intents and purposes for all creation.

Harold G. Koenig, MD, director of the Duke University Medical School's Center for the Study of Religion/Spirituality and Health, writes: "Having a spiritual aspect, then, means that actions are in some way performed to further God's purposes."[7] We have noted elsewhere that ideas about God and divine purposes vary greatly among the world's living religions. But the eternal principle of humankind's duty to obey and love God supremely and to love oneself and others is universal (see [NIV] Deut. 6:5; Lev. 19:18; Luke 10:27). These foundational obligations guide the adherents of all major religions. They determine the direction of life's priorities and the chosen goals of responsible action.

In discussing purposeful living, Koenig makes a helpful distinction between individuals who are physically, emotionally, and spiritually healthy and persons with chronic diseases, illnesses, and disabilities. Consider, for example, the case of a man in his fifties who was forced into premature retirement by an industrial accident. Both of his hands were literally burned to destruction when 12,000 volts of electric current accidentally discharged through his body. Equipped with prosthetic hands, Ken has survived numerous surgeries and adapted positively to his physical confinements. As a Christian believer, he has not lost heart. His confidence in God remains contagious and he serves faithfully as an elder in his congregation.

People with chronic illness and physical disabilities, says Koenig,

> are by no means excluded from experiencing purpose and power. . . . When a person is well and healthy, he or she can be entrapped by goals that have little ultimate meaning or significance. Illness often forces people to reevaluate and shed precious dreams and goals.[8]

He cited a study by Stephanie Carroll on the relationship between spirituality and recovery from alcoholism in a sample of 100 participants in Alcoholics Anonymous.[9] In that study, spirituality was defined as the extent to which the subject practiced step 11—involving prayer and meditation—of the twelve-step program. Carroll found significant positive correlations between the practice of step 11, "purpose in life" scores, and length of sobriety. She concluded that both a sense of purpose in life and maintenance of sobriety are associated with higher scores on spiritual activities such as prayer and meditation.

Faith in and obedience of God are definitely linked to the transformation of one's employment-driven habits into the retiree's purpose-driven life. Rather than transitioning into inactivity and self-preoccupation, carefully chosen priorities can enhance life's meaning and significance. Although your priorities are shaped both by spiritual sensitivity and human limitations, you can transcend self-absorption with a life of service. This prompts us to consider volunteering as one way to achieve a healthy balance, to feel personal worth, and to achieve community usefulness.

VOLUNTEERING

Volunteering is a freely given action of an individual's time, talent, financial resources, or a combination of such assets in behalf of other persons, agencies, institutions, or causes with the intent of meeting a recognized need, stabilizing a disrupted situation, or providing assistance, resources, encouragement, or healing to enhance others' existence. Such informal or formal services are performed in different settings, on a dependable, enduring basis, without charge or constraint. Individuals often join groups of other volunteers, as in the house construction projects of Habitat for Humanity, to pool resources, time, and energies to accomplish a helpful goal.

I spoke with a volunteer who works in a major medical center one day a week, assisting the cardiac nursing staff in pre- and postoperative guidance for heart surgery patients. For patients facing heart surgery, who have been diagnosed with arterial blockage or damage, he shows a brief video on the scheduled surgical procedure to inform the patient and allay his or her anxiety. Having experienced heart by-pass surgery himself, he knows how important the patient's understanding of the surgical process can be. If a surgeon knew, for example, that a patient was convinced he or she would die on the operating table, surgery might not be performed at that time, and careful postoperative monitoring is essential.

Members of my faith community's Bible study group render volunteer services as varied as tutoring children in after-school programs, arranging gifts in a mission house, and distributing provisions each week to low-income families. They serve on the board of the local Salvation Army chapter, provide home furnishings for internationals who have moved into our city, "adopt" students from a nearby university for home visits during the academic year, and deliver Meals on Wheels for the at-home-alone elderly. Such enduring, charitable service is different from membership in a civic club, which may be self-serving in motive.

Some congregations provide formal training of lay care providers, through programs affiliated with groups such as Stephen's Ministries of St. Louis, Missouri. Laypersons are guided in how to be present, prayerful, and facilitative with persons experiencing some difficult, unexpected event. Such crises can turn an individual's world upside down. In fact, an entire family is often affected by one member's addiction, illness, disease, accident, or disability. When people are forced to travel life's unchosen paths, they may feel confused, disconnected, frustrated, powerless, grief-stricken, or anxious.

Whole regions, even nations, can be propelled into horrors of war or oft-fatal infections such as AIDS. People facing natural disasters—whether the devastation of a typhoon in Taiwan, a forest fire in Nevada, a hurricane in Florida, a tornado in Kansas, or starvation in Sudan—require mobilized help. Although a major agency like the International Red Cross may provide logistical assistance, volunteers may help by supplying basic survival needs to care receivers—doing the most simple things, such as "giving a cup of cold water" in the spirit of Christ.

Our religious faith reminds us that divine Providence moves in close when people's worlds collapse. Thus, the volunteer represents more than himself or herself. A helper with altruistic motives symbolizes God's reality and presence when natural disasters—such as Hurricanes Katrina and Rita—strike. When crises come, the lenses of people's souls may open to spiritual reality. Profound hurts remind us of what is truly important as we seek balance in life. "The seeds of lasting faith, hope, and love are often planted in the early hours following a trauma. Who was there? What was said and done? Who sat [with me] in the silence, read from a Psalm, or uttered a simple prayer?"[10] Caring events touch the heart and are cherished and remembered, at least by some recipients of unselfish generosity. Uncommon expressions of volunteerism may involve multitudes of helpers, transcend individual deeds, and unite citizens of many nations in global efforts.

There is often a payoff beyond altruism for persons who perform volunteer services. Linda Fried directs the Center on Aging and Health at Johns Hopkins University. Fried studied physically challenged Experience Corps volunteers in Baltimore and found, among other things, that 50 percent of her sample group grew strong enough to stop using canes within two years after joining a tutoring group.[11] Elderly volunteers demonstrate a decrease in depression and an increase in overall health, and they live longer than their nonvolunteering peers, according to a University of Michigan study.

STAYING WELL

People seeking balance recognize the need for wellness in body, mind, and spirit. I first became interested in the effects of stress on health maintenance and disease processes while experiencing the demands of juggling doctoral studies, professional responsibilities, and family interactions in the 1950s. The best available guides then were in publications such as those by Hans Selye, Director of the Institute of Experimental Medicine and Surgery at the University of Montreal, and in studies like the "Social Readjustment Rating Scale," developed by psychiatrists Thomas Holmes and Richard Rahe of the University of Washington Medical School.[12]

The Significance of Stress

The Holmes-Rahe scale placed numerical stressor-weighted equivalents alongside forty-three life events. Potentially stressful situations were rated on a scale from 11 to 100, with "death of one's spouse" highest. For a person who scored over 300 stress points on the scale, Holmes and Rahe noted a high risk potential for developing major illness within the following two-year period. Stress did not cause the illness, Holmes emphasized, but excessive stressors seemed to promote the disease process.

At about the same time, Archibald Hart, a South African engineer, came to the United States for advanced study, but switched fields to psychology. Before he retired from teaching, Hart published an influential study titled *The Hidden Link Between Adrenalin and Stress.* Having attended a workshop Hart conducted, I am in his debt for citing three effects on our bodies from chronic stress.[13]

1. The immune system, designed to ward off disease and infection, becomes depleted. When stressors continue unabated, the body fails to fight off infections and to prevent disorders like cancer, diabetes, and rheumatoid arthritis.
2. While eustress (good stress resulting from endorphins coming to our rescue in acute stressful situations, like accidents) may be beneficial, chronic stress depletes the body's anti-pain system. When the brain's pain-killing endorphins are depleted, a person's pain tolerance level decreases. Physical and emotional suffering ensue.
3. Just as the brain has endorphins to prevent pain, it also has its own tranquilizers to lower anxiety. Under prolonged stress, this natural defense system is damaged and feelings of anxiety increase. Anxiety, unlike fear that hangs onto an object, is free-floating and leads to increased tension, worry, and inability to focus or relax.

According to a major new study, the causes of heart disease are surprisingly the same in every region and race, and stress seems to play a more important role in heart attacks than was previously recognized. The research, presented at the annual meeting of the European Society of Cardiology, in Munich, Germany, followed 29,000 people in fifty-two countries. It took a decade and 262 scientists to complete the work.[14] The good news: scientists have concluded that 90 percent of the risk factors for heart attacks may be averted. The bad news: a bad cholesterol profile was the most important risk factor in heart disease. Stress came next, followed by improper diet and lack of exercise.

Of major concern to you as a retiree is the seriousness of stress in daily living. The problem, researchers observed, is psychological, not physical, stress—things such as tension at home or at work, financial problems, divorce, losing a child, or feeling the loss of control. Inactivity and improper diet increase the likelihood of obesity, which leads to maladies such as diabetes and heart disease. To help keep stress under control, try some of these stress-reducing suggestions from the Mayo Clinic:

1. Try going to bed thirty minutes early. At least, get plenty of sleep.
2. Read a good book. I would add, listen to relaxing music.
3. Seek out positive people, and limit your activities with negative people.
4. Meditate or pray. I would add, practice worship on a regular basis.
5. Deal with one thing at a time. Delay or delegate an *optional* work project.
6. See a humorous or uplifting movie. Enjoy a spectator sport on television.
7. Tackle all of your unpleasant tasks early in the day; get them over with.
8. Eat properly and exercise regularly (discussed in the following section).
9. Go with the flow. Not every battle has to be won—or even fought. As your mother told you, "Pick your battles wisely. . . ."
10. Ask for help! Get another view of the situation when you are feeling overwhelmed. Share your burden with a friend or a professional counselor.[15]

Learn a new skill, such as using a computer. I have a professor friend who, during one academic year, taught himself to play the flute. During a current sabbatical leave, along with research and writing, he is learning to play the piano. He also plans an international research trip to pursue a topic of interest. Involvement in some educational activity may provide you an opportunity to learn and grow, as well as to contribute something useful to the larger community.

The Importance of Exercise and Diet

We keep life in balance when we remember our unitary nature—body, mind, spirit—and practice wise habits of self-care, such as proper diet and exercise. Because I have heart disease, I participate in a monitored fitness program three days a week at the Harris Medical

Center in our city. My wife and I each have regular physical examinations at a nationally recognized medical center. My HDL (good cholesterol) level is historically low. Because the amount of cholesterol appears hereditary, I maintain a prescribed regimen in order to enhance a healthy HDL/LDL cholesterol profile. Because of an angina experience in 2003, I have learned how important at least a 40+ HDL reading is in plaque formation and management.

Keeping life in balance among Asians has an ancient tradition, mentioned in Chinese chronicles as early as 122 BC. Some years ago, when my wife and I lived in a Hong Kong high-rise apartment, we viewed Chinese men and women daily performing Tai Chi exercises on the roof of a six-story building below. There are some interesting inspirational ideas for the movement philosophy of Tai Chi in the Taoist writings of Chuang Tzu.[16] For example, "the pure man of old slept without dreams and woke without anxiety. He ate without indulging in sweet tastes and breathed deep breaths. The pure man draws breaths from the depths of his heels; the multitude only from their throats." Again, "[The sage] would not lean forward or backward to accommodate [things]. This is called tranquility, [which means] that it is especially in the midst of disturbance that tranquility becomes perfect."

Tai Chi principles are wed to spiritual forces and invoke the harmonizing influence of yin-yang and Eternal Change. The principles of yielding, softness, centeredness, slowness, balance, suppleness, and rootedness are all elements of Taoist philosophy. Tai Chi exercises relate both to fitness in health and to its martial arts applications.

Today, exercise buffs employ many practices to burn excess calories, strengthen muscles, enhance breathing, and foster wellness. Methods range from walking, jogging, bicycling, swimming, weight lifting, stretching, and skating, to mountain climbing, playing musical instruments, and engaging in sports such as golf, bowling, softball, soccer, and volleyball. The amount of one's physical energy and exertion depends on one's age, desire, and degree of fitness. It is wise to seek medical monitoring of the intensity of exercise at the outset of any regimen.

Healthy eating, like proper exercise, depends on variables such as a person's gender, genetic givens, body size, age, health history, and activity level. Americans enjoy a much more opulent lifestyle than residents of many countries in the Earth. We live in a nation of plenty.

Much of labor's drudgery has been removed from work by automation and technology. Inactivity among a majority of overnourished citizens, plus the availability of fast foods and sweets, has produced an alarming statistic. Today, one out of three Americans is overweight.

Scientists tell us that obesity is linked to a person's body mass index, or BMI, a . . . calculation in which your weight is divided by your height. If your BMI is 25, you're overweight. If it's 30 you're obese. Health is jeopardized for persons with an over 30 body mass index. Research reveals that being overweight is associated with 400,000 deaths a year and an increased risk of heart disease, type 2 diabetes, and colon, breast, and other types of cancer.[17] Understandably, many overweight persons feel stigmatized by their obesity and are sensitive about it.

Enormously successful businesses such as Weight Watchers; diets proposed by gurus such as the late Robert Atkins or the South Beach Diet; sports and health clubs; the dietary food supplement and vitamin industries; video fitness programs; along with risky procedures, like gastric bypass [Bariatric] surgery, have become commonplace. Bypass operations were performed on 103,200 patients in one recent year. Such medical procedures carry a level of risk, amid some failures, even deaths.

Some authorities say the math is simple—calories in versus calories out. It takes 3,500 calories to equal one pound of fat. The more calories a person consumes, from whatever food group or indulgence, the more active they must become to maintain a constant weight. To lose weight, a person must burn off more calories than he or she consumes. We tend to assume that people who overeat simply lack willpower, writes Cathy Newman. "What seems increasingly clear, however, is that the drive to overeat has strong biological underpinnings." This implies that food and slow metabolism are not the only culprits in obesity. Rather, people who are genetically disposed to obesity, "may have a stronger biological drive to eat, especially in an environment where food is . . . cheap and plentiful."[18]

Appropriate food portions, for one's age and health history, from the five food groups—grain products, vegetables, fruits, meat and beans, and milk—should form the basis for a healthy diet. Retirees will notice, as they grow older, that their metabolism slows, increasing the likelihood of weight gain. A person does not need to consume the same quantities of food at age fifty-five or sixty as when he or she was eighteen or twenty. Dieticians suggest that your diet should match your medical profile. A retiree's diet should be based on the kinds of physical conditions a person has—such as diabetes, elevated blood pressure, kidney stones, or constipation.[19] Staying well must take into account the significance of stress and its management, along with careful monitoring of diet and an appropriate exercise regimen.

To summarize, as a retiree concerned with your own health and well-being (plus a host of other matters), I have advocated that you pursue life with purpose. Whether you left paid employment of your own volition or were obliged to "hang it up" for any one of many reasons, your calling now is to care for yourself and those closest to you. You and I live in a society that moves at warp speed. We are besieged by many choices. I trust that as you persevered in reading these pages you found the ideas informative, inspiring, and life changing. At least that was my goal. I believe in you, dear reader, and trust that you will BE (or become) a real person by choosing life at its best.

A SUMMARY OF KEY POINTS

- We have observed how retirement changes (almost) everything in our lives and in the experiences of people around us. Changes call for choices and decisions.
- Gaining and maintaining a healthy balance is a prevailing personal challenge in the Western world. Retired persons are not immune from the struggle between former life patterns and changing new demands.
- Volunteering is a profoundly significant way to get oneself off of one's hands and into social interaction with others. The goal is durable service to another person or entity with no thought of personal reward. Giving of oneself in service to others requires courage, sacrifice, and generosity in response to a higher calling.
- Life balance includes staying fit, eating wisely, exercising within the limits of your health history, with regular medical checkups to determine your present health profile, monitor medications, and practice preventive care.
- In the future, your calling is to BE a real person and to choose wisely the path you will follow into the Caller's tomorrows. Choose well. Stay well. Live well.

Appendix for Caregivers:
The Art of Supportive Conversations

Caring persons who sojourn alongside fellow strugglers often search for the right word or appropriate response after hearing of someone's trouble or heartcry. What do you say, for example, when a friend calls to report she's lost her job? How should you respond when someone tearfully confesses her husband's memory confusion: "George has early symptoms of Alzheimer's"? A distinguished community leader dies suddenly following a freak accident. True, the accident was a stupid mistake on his part—but what do you say to those left behind?

"A family matter has come up," a friend might say, "that prevents our getting together." Listening between the lines reveals a divorce proceeding is underway involving a cherished couple and grandchild. The question arises: "Do I simply say 'I'm sorry,' or ask about chronology of the marital conflict, or push for details about why the couple is divorcing and who's to blame?"

A respected corporate leader learned he had prostate cancer. Because he would be absent from the office at least a fortnight following surgery, he disclosed his situation to his leadership team. Beyond that revelation, however, he found that discussing his health with others only added to the strain. "People didn't know how to react," he said, "so they related stories of people they knew who had survived prostate cancer surgery." Their stories and 'I'm sorry' responses were wearying.

People are not comfortable with another's discomfort, notes Nance Guilmartin, author of *Healing Conversations: What to Say When You Don't Know What to Say.* We want to try to fix what's broken and take the pain away from persons who are suffering. Often, we offer a knee-jerk reaction such as "Oh, I'm sorry" because it fills the awkward silence. "It's a response that makes you feel you're showing you care," says Guilmartin. "We want to smooth over the moment of pain for both of us. It's out of the best intentions. But it's that automatic response that doesn't make either of you feel comforted."[1] Guilmartin advises people to get their bearings and—this is the tough part—pause. Staying silent may go against our instincts, but it allows the ministry of your presence to take effect.

Spiritual Wisdom for Successful Retirement
Published by The Haworth Press, Inc. 2006. All rights reserved.
doi:10.1300/5537_12

When you keep your mouth shut and listen, notes Guilmartin, you have opportunity to identify your own feelings and find words that express those feelings. In conversing with a young friend with whom I had not visited in over a year, for example, I learned he and his wife were new parents of a third child. "Well, what a surprise!" I said invitingly, to which he responded, "It was a surprise for us, too."

Here are some ways to help you respond appropriately and navigate an awkward conversation when supporting someone facing life's inevitable challenges, transitions, and losses—at home, work, or in the community.[2]

- Understand that you don't necessarily understand. You won't ever know exactly how the person is feeling, even if you've experienced a similar situation. Each individual responds to stress, pain, loss, and grief differently.
- Avoid opening with "How are you?" When a person is going through a tough time, he or she may habitually say "fine" when that is not the case. Instead, try something like, "I've been thinking of you. I'm glad to see you," and let the conversation flow from there. Practice listening beyond the words to the person.
- *Listening love is patient and kind.* Your readiness to hear the person out may encourage your silence, but not indifference. Listening attentively is hard work. A gentle touch on the shoulder or, if appropriate, a warm hug may be sufficient for this encounter, followed, perhaps, by a note of sincere concern.
- *Offer specific help.* Avoid saying, "Let me know if there's anything I can do." Such words put the initiative on the sufferer to call for help. If you don't know how to assist in a matter, suggest: "Let me think about it and I'll get back with you." Be resourceful, and make sure you keep your promise.
- *Not everyone shares your religious beliefs.* True believers often promise a hurting person, "I'll pray for you," or "I'll be remembering you." Be sensitive to the hurting person's belief system. It may be best to pray without mentioning it.
- *Keep confidences.* If someone shares a personal issue with you in strictest confidence, honor her or his trust. Your confidant needs a relationship of a trusted motive. If the confessor is betrayed, you both lose capital in caring relations.
- *In cases of death, gain permission to talk about the deceased.* You might ask, "Is this a good time to chat about Lance's death?" Or, say something such as, "I always enjoyed Lance's sense of humor. Would you like to hear a story?" If the grieving survivor is comfortable, proceed; if not, let him or her explain why another time will be better. Feelings after loss are tender. Perhaps you can visit at another time.

Notes

Introduction

1. George Gallup Jr. and D. Michael Lindsay, *Surveying the Religious Landscape: Trends in U.S. Beliefs* (Harrisburg, PA: Morehouse Publishing, 1999), 41-42.

2. Lucy Bregman, "Defining Spirituality: Multiple Uses and Murky Meanings of an Incredibly Popular Term," *The Journal of Pastoral Care & Counseling* (Fall, 2004), 157-167. My position differs markedly from the stance expressed by researchers who claim that spirituality is the intrinsic ability of self-determination, quite apart from a beyond-the-self reference point. See John D. Morgan, "The Existential Quest for Meaning," in Kenneth J. Doka and John Morgan (Eds.), *Death and Spirituality* [Amityville, NY: Baywood Publishing Co., 1991, 8]. In support of a bipolar self-Other view, see Frank Stagg, *Polarities of Human Existence in Biblical Perspective, Revised Edition* (Macon, GA: Smyth & Helwys Publishing, Inc., 1994), 13-30; and Lee Strobel, *The Case for a Creator* (Grand Rapids, MI: Zondervan, 2004).

3. Gallup and Lindsay, Ibid., 23-52.

4. Ibid., 3, 97-117.

5. Harold G. Koenig, MD, *Spirituality in Patient Care: Why, How, When, and What* (Philadelphia and London: Templeton Foundation Press, 2002), 7.

Chapter 1

1. Tom Brokaw, *The Greatest Generation* (New York: Random House, 1998).

2. Peter T. Kilborn, "Alive, Well and on the Prowl; It's the Geriatric Mating Game," *Scottsdale Journal* (March 7, 2004); http://www.nytimes.com/2004/03/04.

3. Ibid.

4. Nancy K. Schlossberg, *Retire Smart, Retire Happy: Finding Your True Path in Life* (New York: American Psychological Association, 2003).

5. Michael D. Yapko, *Hand-Me-Down Blues: How to Stop Depression from Spreading in Families* (New York: St. Martin's Griffin, 1999), 56.

6. "An Evening with Frank McCourt," January 12, 2006. Bass Performance Hall, Fort Worth, Texas. Also Hillel Italic, "A Profile of Frank McCourt," AP National Writer, program notes, the *Star-Telegram,* Forth Worth, Texas.

Chapter 2

1. John P. Newport, *Life's Ultimate Questions: A Contemporary Philosophy of Religion* (Dallas: Word Publishing, 1989), 10.

Spiritual Wisdom for Successful Retirement
Published by The Haworth Press, Inc. 2006. All rights reserved.
doi:10.1300/5537_13

2. Pierre Teilhard de Chardin, *On Happiness* (London: William Collins Sons & Co. Ltd., 1973), 55.

3. Quoted by Mary Hiteman, "Reaping with Shouts of Joy," *Your Daily Appointment with God: Imagine What God Can Do* (Richmond, VA: First Baptist Church, February 22-September 4, 2004), 13.

4. Cited by Robert Powell, "Ready, set, retire: Five steps you must take before you do" (Boston: CBS MarketWatch.com, January 14, 2004), 2.

Chapter 3

1. Andrew D. Lester, *Hope in Pastoral Care and Counseling* (Louisville, KY: Westminster John Knox Press, 1995), 5-8.

2. Charles V. Gerkin, "Pastoral Care and Models of Aging," *Journal of Religion and Aging, 6* (1989), 83-100.

3. Paul W. Pruyser, "Aging: Downward, Upward, or Forward," in Seward Hiltner, ed. *Toward a Theology of Aging* (New York: Human Sciences Press, 1975), 102-118.

4. Erik H. Erikson, "Growth and Crises of the Healthy Personality," in *Identity and the Life Cycle* (New York: International Universities Press, 1959), 50-100.

5. Robert Coles, *Erik H. Erikson: The Growth of His Work* (Boston: Little, Brown and Co., 1970), 132-139.

6. Jurgen Moltmann, *The Theology of Hope*, trans. James W. Leitsch (New York: Harper and Row, 1967).

7. Gerkin, "Pastoral Care," 96.

8. Moltmann, *The Crucified God* (New York: Harper and Row, 1974), 252-255.

9. Rick Warren, *The Purpose-Driven Life: What on Earth Am I Here For?* (Grand Rapids, MI: Zondervan, 2002), 312-319.

10. Jane Ramos Tremble, "Friends Create Unique Retirement-Living, Home," *Star-Telegram* (April 28, 2004), 1, 5-H.

11. Sheryl Garrett, et al., *Just Give Me the Answer$* (Chicago, IL: Dearborn Trade Publishing, 2004; click: www.GarrettPlanningNetwork.com).

12. Related by Glenn Ruffenach, editor of "Encore," *The Wall Street Journal*'s quarterly guide to retirement, in the *Star-Telegram* (June 13, 2004), 4-F.

13. James N. Lapsley, *Renewal in Late Life Through Pastoral Counseling* (Mahwah, NJ: Paulist Press, 1992), 17.

14. See Ken Dychtwald, *Age Wave* (Los Angeles: Jeremy P. Tarker, Inc., 1989); also, *Age Power: How the 21st Century Will Be Ruled by the New Old* (Los Angeles: Jeremy P. Tarker, Inc., 1999).

15. Jimmy Carter, *The Virtues of Aging* (New York: Ballantine, 1998); also, see Douglas Brinkley, *The Unfinished Presidency: Jimmy Carter's Journey Beyond the White House* (New York: Viking Press, 1998).

16. Gene Cohen, *The Creative Age: Awakening Human Potential in the Second Half of Life* (New York: Harper Collins, 2001); also, see David Petty, *Aging Gracefully* (Nashville, TN: Broadman and Holman Publishers, 2003), 135-141.

Chapter 4

1. Viktor E. Frankl, *Man's Search for Meaning: An Introduction to Logotherapy* (New York: Washington Square Press, 1963), 60.
2. Ibid., 142.
3. Lewis Carroll, *The Annotated Alice: Alice's Adventures in Wonderland and Through the Looking Glass* (Cleveland: The World Publishing Co., 1960), 37.
4. *Tarrant Baptist Challenge* (June, 2004), 12.
5. *Star-Telegram* (September 26, 2002), B-1.
6. Eugene H. Peterson, *Working the Angles: The Shape of Pastoral Integrity* (Grand Rapids, MI: William B. Eerdmans Publishing Co., 1988, 1995), 47.
7. Ibid., 46. Cf. Tilden Edwards, *Sabbath Time* (New York: Seabury Press, 1982).
8. Karl Menninger, MD, *Sparks,* ed. by Lucy Freeman (New York: Thomas Y. Crowell Co., 1973), 86-87.
9. Jurgen Moltmann, *In the End—the Beginning: The Life of Hope*; trans. Margaret Kohl from the German *Im Ende—der Anfang* (Minneapolis: Fortress Press, 2004), 88.
10. For an excellent, brief, yet comprehensive theodicy, see James C. Denison, "Tsunamis, Tragedy, and God: Where Is Our Father When His Children Hurt?" *The Word Today: Today's News in Spiritual Perspective;* from subscriptions@ thewordinlife.org (January 7, 2005). Also see, C. W. Brister, *Pastoral Care in the Church,* 3rd. ed. rev. (HarperSanFrancisco, 1992), 2-3.

Chapter 5

1. Trudy Lieberman, "Fatal Mistakes," AARP Bulletin (November 2004), 18-21.
2. Ibid., 19. See also, Rosemary Gibson, et al., *The Wall of Silence: The Untold Story of the Medical Mistakes That Kill and Injure Millions of Americans* (Washington, DC: Lifeline Press, 2003).
3. Lieberman, "Fatal Mistakes," 21.
4. Anthony M. D'Agostino, MD, "Depression: Schism in Contemporary Psychiatry," *American Journal of Psychiatry 132:*6 (1975), 629.
5. Helen Mayberg, MD, cited in the Tufts University "Health & Nutrition Letter" (August 2004), 1, 8.
6. Herbert Anderson and Freda A. Gardner, *Living Alone* (Louisville, KY: Westminister John Knox Press, 1997), 85.
7. Princeton Religion Research Center, *Religion in America* (Princeton, NJ: The Gallup Poll, 1996).
8. Harold G. Koenig, MD, *Spirituality in Patient Care: Why, How, When, and What* (Philadelphia: Templeton Foundation Press, 2002), 7.
9. Dianne Hales, "Why Prayer Could Be Good Medicine," *Parade Magazine* (March 23, 2003), 4-5.
10. Ibid., 4.
11. Ibid., 5.
12. Michael Yapko, *Breaking the Pattern of Depression* (New York: Doubleday, 1997), 161-168.
13. Ibid., 339.

Chapter 6

1. Charles R. Swindoll, *Growing Strong in the Seasons of Life* (Portland, OR: Multnomah Press, 1983), 262-263.
2. Douglas Jehl and David Rohde, "Captured Qaeda Figure Led Way to Information Behind Warning," *The New York Times* (August 2, 2004), ww.nytimes.com /2004/08/02/politics/02intel.html.
3. James C. Denison, Pastor, Park Cities Baptist Church, Dallas, Texas, "Faith at Level Orange," *The Word Today* (August 2, 2004).
4. Steven Lee Myers, "From Anxiety, Fear and Hope, the Deadly Rescue in Moscow," *The New York Times* (November 1, 2002), Archives www.nytimes.com.
5. Hugh Downs, ABC's *20/20* (August, 1993).
6. Sarah A. Butler, *Caring Ministry: A Contemplative Approach to Pastoral Care* (New York: The Continuum Publishing Company, 1999), 88.
7. Ibid., 89-90.

Chapter 7

1. John Donne, "For Whom the Bell Tolls," in Ralph L. Woods, ed., *The Tolling Bell—A Devotion: A Treasury of the Familiar* (New York: The Macmillan Company, 1945), 572.
2. John Bowlby, *Attachment and Loss, Vol. 2* (London: Hogarth Press, 1973), 369.
3. Herbert Anderson and Robert Cotton Fite, *Becoming Married* (Louisville: Westminster John Knox Press, 1993), 115-116. Also, see Louis and Melissa McBurney, *Real Questions, Real Answers About Sex: The Complete Guide to Intimacy As God Intended* (Grand Rapids, MI: Zondervan, 2005).
4. Calvin Miller, *A Covenant for All Seasons: The Marriage Journey* (Wheaton, IL: Harold Shaw Publishers, 1995), vii.
5. See C. S. Lewis, *The Four Loves* (London: Geoffrey Bles, 1960; New York: HBJ Paperback, 1971).
6. C. S. Lewis, *The Joyful Christian* (New York: Macmillan Publishing Co., Inc., 1977), 187.
7. See Elizabeth Raum, *Dietrich Bonhoeffer: Called by God* (New York: Continuum, 2002).

Chapter 8

1. An introduction to *From Here to Eternity*, starring Burt Lancaster, Montgomery Clift, Deborah Kerr, and Donna Reed may be found in the Internet Movie Database at www.imdb.com.
2. John D. Fisher, www.heart-transplant.co.uk., revised December 27, 2003; accessed January 1, 2004.
3. Denise Grady, "Tubes, Pump, and Fragile Hope Keep a Baby's Heart Beating," *The New York Times* (August 22, 2004) Health section; Internet: http://www.nytimes .com/2004/08/22/science/22heart.html?th.

4. Paul Tillich, *The Courage to Be* (New Haven: Yale University Press, 1952), 170.

5. Martin Heidigger, *Sein und Zeit* (1927), trans. by John Macquarrie and Edward Robinson (New York: Harper, 1962).

6. Lewis married Joy Davidman, an excommunist and Jewish-Christian, when she was seriously ill. See *A Grief Observed* (London: Faber and Faber Limited, 1961); published under the pseudonym N. W. Clerk.

7. Sheldon Vanauken, *A Severe Mercy* (San Francisco: Harper and Row Publishers, 1977).

8. Ibid., 177-178.

9. In Mary Samford Laurence, comp., *Treasured Poems That Touch the Heart* (New York: Galahad Books, 1996), 187.

10. David C. Thomasma, "Death," in *World Book Online Reference Center,* http:// www.aolsvc.worldbook.aol.com/ar?/na/ar/co/ar150700,htm, December 18, 2003. Thomasma is a former Professor and Director, Medical Humanities Program, Loyola University Chicago Medical Center.

11. Thomas L. Friedman, "War of Ideas, Part I," *The New York Times* (January 8, 2004); accessed http://www.nytimes.com/2004/01/08/opinion/08FRIE.html.

12. Nigel Wright, Principal, Spurgeon's College, London, Study Paper, Baptist World Alliance Christian Ethics Commission (Seville, Spain: July 8-12, 2002).

13. Zalman Schachter-Shalomi and Ronald S. Miller, *From Age-ing to Sage-ing: A Profound New Vision of Growing Older* (New York: Warner Books, 1995), 165-167.

14. Ibid., 165.

15. Jessica Mitford, *The American Way of Death* (New York: Simon and Schuster, 1963).

16. Studs Terkel, *Will the Circle Be Unbroken? Reflections on Death, Rebirth, and Hunger for a Faith* (New York: Ballantine Books, 2002), xix.

17. Tim O'Brien, *The Things They Carried* (New York: Broadway Books, 1998).

18. Ibid., 225-246.

19. Ibid., 244-245.

20. Alexander Cruden, *Cruden's Complete Concordance* (Grand Rapids, MI: Zondervan Publishing House, 1968; Holt, Rinehart, and Winston, Inc., 1930).

21. Jurgen Moltmann, *In the End—the Beginning: The Life of Hope*; trans. by Margaret Kohl (Minneapolis: Fortress Press, 2004), 45-48.

22. Ibid., 157-158.

23. Ibid., 158.

24. Schachter-Shalomi and Miller, *From Age-ing to Sage-ing,* 54-56.

25. Katherine Fischer, *Winter Grace: Spirituality and Aging* (Nashville: Upper Room Books, 1998), 192. For an individualistic, mythical view of eternity, see Mitch Albom, *The Five People You Meet in Heaven* (New York: Hyperion, 2003).

Chapter 9

1. Christopher Reeve, *Nothing Is Impossible: Reflections on a New Life* (New York: Ballantine, Random House Publishing Group, 2002); see, Adrian Havill, *Man*

of Steel—The Career and Courage of Christopher Reeve (New York: Signet Books, 1996); also see "Incredible Journey," *People* (October 25, 2004), 64.

2. See Studs Terkel, *Will the Circle Be Unbroken? Reflections on Death, Rebirth, and Hunger for a Faith* (New York: Ballantine Books, 2002). In *Change Happens: Finding Your Way Through Life's Transitions* (Macon, GA: Peake Road, 1997), I wrote extensively of family systems factors causing the loss of one's "inner home" and then of our lifelong struggle to be home at last; see pages 73-104.

3. Martin Newman, "Longing to Belong," *The Hong Kong Sunday Morning Post Review* (October 10, 2004), 9.

4. John Patton, *The RSN News: The Newsletter of the Retired Supervisors' Network* (November 2004), n.p.

5. John Weir Perry, *Lord of the Four Quarters* (New York: George Braziller, 1966), cited in Zalman Schachter-Shalomi and Ronald S. Miller, *From Age-ing to Sage-ing* (New York: Warner Books, 1995), 150.

6. Excerpted from a health report by John Schwartz and James Estrin, "Living for Today, Locked in a Paralyzed Body," *The New York Times* (November 7, 2004), Health section, n.p.

7. Ibid.

8. David R. Gergen, "The Power of One," op. ed., *The New York Times* (November 19, 2004).

9. Lucy Freeman, ed., *Karl Menninger, M.D. Sparks* (New York: Thomas Y. Crowell Company, 1973), 86.

10. Hans Selye, *Stress Without Distress* (Philadelphia: J. B. Lippincott Company, 1974), 22.

11. D. Elton Trueblood, *Essays in Gratitude* (Nashville: Broadman Press, 1982), 10.

12. Edward E. Thornton, *Being Transformed: An Inner Way of Spiritual Growth* (Philadelphia: The Westminster Press, 1984), 102-103.

13. Harold G. Koenig, *Purpose and Power in Retirement: New Opportunities for Meaning and Significance* (Philadelphia: Templeton Foundation Press, 2002), 96-114.

14. Bob Buford, *Finishing Well: What People Who REALLY Live Do Differently* (Nashville: Integrity Publishers, 2004).

Chapter 10

1. Alan Robinson, AP Sports. "Gardner Stunned in Overtime of Wrestling Semifinal," http://aolsvc.news.aol.com/sports/article.adp?id=2004082504390999002 and _cc=2andcid=942.

2. Abraham J. Heschel, *God in Search of Man* (New York: Meridian, 1959), 200-230.

3. Rushworth M. Kidder, *How Good People Make Tough Choices* (New York: Fireside Division, Simon and Schuster, 1996), 218-219.

4. Ibid., 109-150; see especially 220-221.

5. Richard and Linda Eyre, *Lifebalance* (New York: Ballantine Books, 1987), 15.

6. Ibid. Paraphrased from N. Larry Baker, pastor, First Baptist Church, Sun City West, Arizona, in a sermon August 15, 2004: "Keeping Life in Balance." The author

is indebted to Baker for introducing this concept and permitting inclusion of his ideas.

7. Harold G. Koenig, MD, *Purpose and Power in Retirement: New Opportunities for Meaning and Significance* (Radnor, PA: Templeton Foundation Press, 2002), 63; cf. 71-95.

8. Ibid., 65.

9. Stephanie Carroll, "Spirituality and Purpose in Life in Alcoholism Recovery," *Journal of Studies on Alcohol 54,* (3) (1993), 297-301; cited by Koenig, 67.

10. Sarah A. Butler, *Caring Ministry: A Contemplative Approach to Pastoral Care* (New York Continuum, 1999), 98.

11. Angie C. Marek, "50 Ways to Fix Your Life—#48 Volunteer," *U. S. News and World Report* (January 3, 2005), 84.

12. Hans Selye, *The Physiology and Pathology of Exposure to Stress* (Montreal: Acta, Inc., 1950); *The Stress of Life* (New York: McGraw Hill, 1956); *Stress Without Distress* (Philadelphia and New York: J. B. Lippincott Co., 1974). Cf. T. H. Holmes and R. H. Rahe, "The Social Rating Scale," *Journal of Psychosomatic Research* (11) (1967), 213-218.

13. Archibald D. Hart, *The Hidden Link Between Adrenalin and Stress* (Waco: Word Books, 1986), 80-81.

14. "No Bounds Found for Heart Disease," Associated Press (August 29, 2004).

15. See excellent ideas for reducing stress in Koenig, *Purpose and Power,* 142-150.

16. "Tai Chi," http://www.chebucto.ns.ca/Philosophy/Taichi/tao-chi.html.

17. See the major report on the cost of fat by Cathy Newman, "Why Are We So Fat?" *National Geographic 206* (2) (August 2004), 46-61.

18. Ibid.

19. Koenig, *Purpose and Power,* 154-156.

Appendix

1. Nance Guilmartin, *Healing Conversations: What to Say When You Don't Know What to Say* (San Francisco: Jossey-Bass, Inc., 2002).

2. Laura Velicer, "Healing Ways," *The South China Morning Post* (October 25, 2004), C-6. Several suggestions in the Appendix are indebted to Ms. Velicer's substantive essay.

Resources

Books

Albom, Mitch. *Tuesdays with Morrie: An Old Man, a Young Man, and Life's Greatest Lesson.* New York: Doubleday, 1997.

Anderson, Herbert and Freda A. Gardner. *Living Alone.* Louisville, KY: Westminster John Knox Press, 1997.

Barnes, Craig. *Searching for Home: Spirituality for Restless Souls.* Grand Rapids, MI: Baker/Brazos, 2004.

Brakeman, Lyn. *The God Between: A Spirituality of Relationships.* Philadelphia: Innisfree Press, 2001.

Bridges, William. *Transitions: Making Sense of Life's Changes.* Reading, MA: Addison-Wesley, 1980. See also *Managing Transitions: Making the Most of Change.* Reading, MA: Addison-Wesley, 1991.

Brister, C. W. *Change Happens: Finding Your Way Through Life's Transitions.* Macon, GA: Peake Road, 1997. See also *Pastoral Care in the Church,* Third Edition, revised. San Francisco: HarperSanFrancisco, 1992.

Buford, Bob. *Finishing Well: What People Who REALLY Live Do Differently.* Nashville: Integrity Publishers, 2004. See also *Halftime: Changing Your Game Plan from Success to Significance.* Grand Rapids, MI: Zondervan, 1994.

Butler, Sarah A. *Caring Ministry: A Contemplative Approach to Pastoral Care.* New York: Continuum, 1999.

Carter, Jimmy. *The Virtues of Aging.* New York: The Ballantine Publishing Group, 1998.

Covey, Stephen R. *First Things First: To Live, to Love, to Learn, to Leave a Legacy.* New York: Simon and Schuster, 1994.

Dayringer, Richard. *Life Cycle: Psychological and Theological Perceptions.* Binghamton, NY: The Haworth Pastoral Press, 2000.

Driskill, J. Lawrence. *Adventures in Senior Living: Learning How to Make Retirement Meaningful and Enjoyable.* Binghamton, NY: The Haworth Pastoral Press, 1997.

Fischer, Kathleen. *Winter Grace: Spirituality and Aging.* Nashville: Upper Room Books, 1998.

Friedman, Edwin. *Generation to Generation: Family Process in Church and Synagogue.* New York: Guilford Press, 1985.

Spiritual Wisdom for Successful Retirement
Published by The Haworth Press, Inc. 2006. All rights reserved.
doi:10.1300/5537_14

Gilligan, Carol. *In a Different Voice*. Cambridge, MA: Harvard University Press, 1981.

Gould, Roger. *Transformations: Growth and Change in the Adult Years*. New York: Simon and Schuster, 1978.

Greer, Jane. *Gridlock: Finding the Courage to Move on in Love, Work, and Life*. New York: Doubleday, 2000.

Grimes, Ronald L. *Deeply into the Bone: Re-inventing Rites of Passage*. Berkley, CA: University of California Press, 2000.

Guinness, Os. *The Call: Finding and Fulfilling the Central Purpose of Your Life*. Nashville: Thomas Nelson's W Publishing Group, 2003.

Gutowski, Carolyn. *Grandparents Are Forever*. Mahwah, NJ: Paulist Press, 1994.

Harvey, John H. *Give Sorrow Words: Perspectives on Loss and Trauma*. Philadelphia: Brunner/Mazel, 2000.

Heckler, Richard A. *Crossings: Everyday People, Unexpected Events, and Life-Affirming Change*. New York: Harcourt, Brace and Company, 1998.

Heschel, Abraham J. *The Sabbath: Its Meaning for Modern Man*. New York: Farrar, Straus and Giroux, 1985.

Kaufman, Sharon R. *The Ageless Self: Sources of Meaning in Late Life*. Madison, WI: University of Wisconsin Press, 1986.

Kirkland, Kevin and Howard McIlveen. *Full Circle: Spirituality Therapy for the Elderly*. Binghamton, NY: The Haworth Press, 1998.

Koenig, Harold G., MD, *Purpose and Power in Retirement: New Opportunities for Meaning and Significance*. Philadelphia: Templeton Foundation Press, 2002; *Spirituality in Patient Care*; see also *A Gospel for the Mature Years: Finding Fulfillment by Knowing and Using Your Gifts*. Binghamton, NY: The Haworth Pastoral Press, 1997.

Kotre, John and Elizabeth Hall. *Seasons of Life: Our Dramatic Journey from Birth to Death*. Boston: Little, Brown, and Co., 1990.

Lapsley, James N. *Renewal in Late Life Through Pastoral Counseling*. Mahwah, NJ: Paulist Press, 1992.

Lester, Andrew D. *The Angry Christian: A Theology for Care and Counseling*. Louisville, KY: Westminster John Knox Press, 2003. See also *Hope in Pastoral Care and Counseling*, Ibid., 1995.

Leuwen, Larry Steward Van. *Gender and Grace: Love, Work, and Parenting in a Changing World*. Downers Grove, IL: InterVarsity Press, 1990.

Levinson, Daniel J. et al. *The Seasons of a Man's Life*. New York: Alfred A. Knopf, 1978. See also Levinson, Daniel J. and Judy D. Levinson, *The Seasons of a Woman's Life*. New York: Ballantine, 1996.

Moltmann, Jurgen. *In the End—The Beginning: The Life of Hope*. Minneapolis: Fortress Press, 2004.

Morgan, Richard L. *I Never Found That Rocking Chair: God's Call at Retirement*. Nashville: Upper Room Books, 1992.

Muller, Wayne. *Sabbath: Restoring the Sacred Rhythm of Rest.* New York: Bantam Books, 1999.

Parks, Sharon. *The Critical Years: The Young Adult's Search for a Faith to Live By.* San Francisco: Harper and Row, 1986.

Peck, M. Scott. *In Search of Stones: A Pilgrimage of Faith, Reason, and Discovery.* New York: Hyperion, 1995.

Petty, David L. *Aging Gracefully: Keeping the Joy in the Journey.* Nashville: Broadman and Holman Publishers, 2003.

Roof, Wade Clark. *A Generation of Seekers.* San Francisco: HarperSanFrancisco, 1993.

Schachter-Shalomi, Zalman and Ronald S. Miller. *From Age-ing to Sage-ing: A Profound New Vision of Growing Older.* New York: Warner Books, 1995.

Schipani, Daniel S. *The Way of Wisdom in Pastoral Counseling.* Elkhart, IN: Institute of Mennonite Studies, 2003.

Schlossberg, Nancy K. *Retire Smart, Retire Happy: Finding Your True Path in Life.* New York: American Psychological Association, 2003.

Sheehy, Gail. *Understanding Men's Passages.* New York: Random House, 1998. See also *New Passages: Mapping Your Life Across Time.* New York: Ballantine, 1995.

Srode, Molly. *Creating a Spiritual Retirement: A Guide to the Unseen Possibilities in Our Lives.* Woodstock, VT: Skylight Paths Publishing, 2003.

Stevenson-Moessner, Jeanne, ed. *In Her Own Time: Women and Developmental Issues in Pastoral Care.* Minneapolis: Fortress Press, 2000.

Strasser, Steven and John Sena. *Transitions: Successful Strategies from Mid-Career to Retirement.* Hawthorne, NJ: Career Press, 1992.

Sullender, R. Scott. *Losses in Later Life: A New Way of Walking with God,* Second Edition. New York: The Haworth Pastoral Press, 1998.

Sullivan, Betty Anne. *Spiritual Elders: Women of Worth in the Third Millennium.* Brockton, MA: Brockton Publishing Company, 1999.

Swindoll, Charles R. *Growing Strong in the Seasons of Life.* Portland: Multnomah Press, 1983.

Terkel, Studs. *Working: People Talk about What They Do All Day and How They Feel About What They Do.* New York: The New Press, 1972. See also *Will the Circle Be Unbroken? Reflections on Death, Rebirth, and Hunger for a Faith.* New York: The New Press, 2001.

Trueblood, D. Elton. *Essays in Gratitude.* Nashville: Broadman Press, 1982.

Viorst, Judith. *Necessary Losses.* New York: Ballantine, 1986.

Warren, Rick. *The Purpose Driven Life: What on Earth Am I Here For?* Grand Rapids, MI: Zondervan, 2002.

Weaver, Andrew, Harold G. Koenig, and Phyllis C. Roe, eds. *Reflections on Aging and Spiritual Growth.* Nashville: Abingdon Press, 1998.

Willard, Dallas. *Renovation of the Heart: Putting on the Character of Christ.* Colorado Springs: NavPress, 2002. See also *The Spirit of the Disciplines: Understanding How God Changes Lives.* New York: HarperCollins, 1988.

Yapko, Michael D. *Breaking the Patterns of Depression.* New York: Doubleday, 1997. See also *Hand-Me-Down Blues: How to Stop Depression from Spreading in Families.* New York: St. Martin's Griffin, 1999.

Web Sites

www.aahomecare.org: Industry information for homecare providers.

www.aarp.org: AARP retirement information for you and your family.

www.businessweek.com/bwdaily/dnflash/...2004/nf20040917_8121_db026.htm: Finding lost retirement financial assets.

www.caremangers.org: Personal caregiver resources from the National Association of Professional Geriatric Care Managers.

www.HappilyRetired.com: Retirement preparation—health and finances.

www.hr.arizona.edu/07_sep/retire/: Intentional retirement planning, Human Resources Retirement Resources home page.

www.humanresources.about.com/od/retirement401k/index_a.htm: Retirement savings options—401(k) plans, IRAs, Roths, and information on Social Security.

www.ipers.org/links.htm: Planning for retirement, resources from the American Savings Education Council.

www.librarysupportstaff.com/retirementtips.html: Researching retirement communities and planning for assisted living.

www.medicare.gov/hhcompare/home.asp: For a list of providers.

www.taxtopics.net: An index of tax resources on the Internet—property tax, qualified tuition plans (529), railroad retirement, and indices.

www.taxtopics.net/retirement.htm: Added tax guides and planning tips.

Sponsored Links

www.creativeretirement.org: Creative retirement, activities, job hunting, books.

www.Retire-4-life.com: Plan your retirement now.

www.Retirement1.net: Comprehensive retirement information.

Index

Spiritual Wisdom for Successful Retirement
Published by The Haworth Press, Inc. 2006. All rights reserved.
doi:10.1300/5537_15